Fifty-Five Years with Russia

Studies in Russian and Slavic Literatures, Cultures, and History

Series Editor
Lazar Fleishman (Stanford University)

Fifty-Five Years with Russia

MAGNUS LJUNGGREN

Translated by
CHARLES ROUGLE

Boston
2016

Library of Congress Cataloging-in-Publication Data

Names: Ljunggren, Magnus, author.

Title: Fifty-five years with Russia / Magnus Ljunggren ; translated by Charles Rougle.

Other titles: Mina 55 êar med Ryssland. English

Description: Boston : Academic Studies Press, 2016.

Series: Studies in Russian and Slavic literatures, cultures, and history

Identifiers: LCCN 2016037761 (print) | LCCN 2016040376 (ebook) | ISBN 9781618115386 (paperback) | ISBN 9781618115393 (digital) | ISBN 9781618115393 (e-book)

Subjects: LCSH: Ljunggren, Magnus. | Russian literature—Study and teaching. | Soviet literature—Study and teaching. | Litterateurs—Sweden—Biography. | Slavists—Sweden—Biography. | Scholars—Sweden—Biography. | Soviet Union—Intellectual life. | Russia (Federation)—Intellectual life. | Intellectuals—Soviet Union—Biography. | Intellectuals—Russia (Federation)—Biography.

BISAC: BIOGRAPHY & AUTOBIOGRAPHY / Literary. | HISTORY / Europe / Russia & the Former Soviet Union.

Classification: LCC PG2947.L65 A313 2016 (print) | LCC PG2947.L65 (ebook) | DDC 891.709—dc23 LC record available at https://lccn.loc.gov/2016037761 ISBN 978-1-61811-538-6 (hardback)

ISBN 978-1-61811-539-3 (electronic)
©Academic Studies Press, 2016
Book design by Kryon Publishing,
www.kryonpublishing.com

Published by Academic Studies Press
28 Montfern Avenue
Brighton, MA 02135, USA
press@academicstudiespress.com
www.academicstudiespress.com

Fifty-Five Years with Russia

To put it directly, I have lived my entire adult life with two native countries: Sweden and Russia. This is what I want to talk about.

So how exactly did it all start? Well, it all began in 1961 when upon graduation from high school I entered the Armed Forces Language School in Uppsala as pretty much a blank page. There in an old barracks I spent a very effective year studying Russian under an extremely challenging instructor and surrounded by a stimulating circle of friends. My life took a new turn under the enchantment of the Russian language and Russian culture.

After Basic Training, at the age of nineteen a friend and I traveled by car through France. This was in the summer of 1962. On a Mediterranean beach in Juan les Pins I read Nils Åke Nilsson's *Soviet Russian Literature 1917–1947*. It was an important experience. The book spoke to me, telling me about a strange Soviet, occasionally Stalinist reality. Society and literature in intimate association. Nilsson had a talent for explaining all these difficult topics with artless simplicity. I believe I wanted to follow in his footsteps and become an interpreter of all things Russian.

Soon it was time to get some academic qualifications. There in the old building on Drottninggatan in Stockholm that housed the Russian Institute Nilsson became my warmly appreciated instructor in Russian literature. He had just published an article in the journal *Ord & Bild* about Yevgeny Yevtushenko and his famous poem about the taboo but vigorous anti-Semitism that banned even the mention of the Nazi massacre at Babi Yar. We had worked our way through it already when it was first published in September 1961. Now in the early autumn of 1962 he issued his prophetic poetic word of warning against Stalin's heirs. And a few months after that the time had come for Alexander Solzhenitsyn to make his sensational debut with *One Day in the Life of Ivan Denisovich*.

Just then I was working on my own article about Yevtushenko, stressing even more than Nilsson had done his rebellious spirit. Soon I was reading everything I could get my hands on about the subject in the archives of the old Klara district newspaper offices in downtown Stockholm.

It was as though the shoots of freedom that had sprouted in the post-Stalinist Thaw were entwined with my own personal growth. The whole world seemed to be in the throes of flux, and I turned twenty. It was the age of Kennedy, the Beatles, and Bob Dylan: "The times they are a'changing." Although I was mostly looking eastward.

I soon came into contact with a journalist my age, who had just started the cultural magazine *Origo*. Its first issue in a newly revamped format appeared in early 1963 and carried my Yevtushenko essay. But something was going on in the middle of all the euphoria. In March 1963 Khrushchev called Soviet writers and artists on the carpet in a speech he gave in the Kremlin. The pendulum was swinging back. Stalin's heirs were brooding on revenge. *Origo*'s third issue that year published my article on Alexander Yesenin-Volpin, Valery Tarsis, and Mikhail Naritsa, three Russian writers who for political reasons had been committed to mental hospitals. Referring to poems by Yesenin-Volpin published in the United States, I emphasized his powerful yearning for freedom: "One goal is clear / an insane goal: freedom!"

I had already begun my journalistic career, and at times I could be a bit forward. In early September I had made my debut on the cultural page of the daily *Expressen* in the form of a full-page interview with the Soviet playwright Anatoly Sofronov during his visit to Stockholm. Just to be on the safe side, since I didn't want to risk being refused a visa, I signed it as "Bertil Block." Bertil is my middle name, and I took Block from Alexander Blok. It was originally *Expressen* cultural editor Bo Strömstedt's idea. "Block" just seemed natural, since I'd heard that a couple of years earlier he had published a contribution on a Russian theme by someone signing as "Karl Erik Mandelstam." Osip Mandelstam's poetry was just beginning to be rediscovered in the West, and it is tempting to guess that it was none other than Nils Åke Nilsson who had come upon this clever way to conceal his identity.

The story behind my interview was as follows. The émigré newspaper *Nashe obshchee delo* had recently published a letter from an anonymous Soviet Russian claiming Sofronov was a graphomaniac who had made a career during Stalin's final years by ruthlessly denouncing and eliminating more talented colleagues. He gradually usurped enormous power over literature, and he used it after Stalin as well to stifle creative originality. The letter, which we later learned was written by the prominent and earlier "repressed" literary scholar Yulian Oksman, was in reality a cry for help. Sofronov's circle of hack writers was about to get their revenge on Yevtushenko, Solzhenitsyn, and everything else that was new.

Oksman drew special attention to the case of the children's author Nadezhda Nadezhdina. In 1950 she had been sentenced to eight years' hard labor on the basis of a denunciation by Sofronov, who had discovered that she once had been expelled from the Komsomol for doubting Stalin's brilliance. Parenthetically, it turned out that Sofronov's slander of Nadezhdina was actually aimed at her teacher Samuil Marshak, in the context of the late Stalinist anti-cosmopolitan campaign. Thus, Sofronov was a rabid anti-Semite.

Now I got it into my head that I would take a closer look at Sofronov. With no authority whatever, I set off for the offices of the Swedish Writers' Union in Stockholm, where the visiting Soviet writers had convened a press conference. After the reporters from *Dagens Nyheter* and *Stockholms-Tidningen* had asked their polite questions I jumped in. First, I wondered whether we could regard 1956 as a borderline in Soviet literature. Sofronov didn't think so. Boundaries arise when a great new talent emerges. Was Alexander Solzhenitsyn such a talent? No, Sofronov explained. The newcomer had attracted a lot of attention, but he was already beginning to fade. "He has to learn to understand life in all its depth." And with that the Stalinist had put the former camp prisoner in his place.

Finally, I asked my main question: "What do you think of Nadezhda Nadezhdina's writing?" Silence. For a brief moment he seemed slightly confused. Then he collected his wits and, considering that snitching was his profession, exclaimed with remarkable ambiguity: "There are five thousand writers in the Soviet Union. Surely you realize that I can't keep track of them all."

Fairly soon a translation of the interview appeared in *Nashe obshchee delo*, so to some extent it must have also trickled into the Soviet Union. It won me praise from our old émigré instructor Sergei Rittenberg, himself a Petersburg Jew like Oksman, but just a few years younger. He gave us conversation exercises in his refined, old-fashioned Russian and exciting reports on his summertime visits to Leningrad, where among other things he called on Anna Akhmatova.

Soon I wrote a review for *Expressen* of Vasily Aksyonov's novel *Ticket to the Stars*, which had just been translated into Swedish. With its portrayal of young people during the Thaw who in every way they could tried to liberate themselves from dogmas and coercion, its basic theme was freedom. It was not for nothing that Aksyonov was among the writers whom Khrushchev attacked in his harangue.

I continued working for *Origo*, writing pieces such as an interview with Mikhail Sholokhov when he visited Stockholm. He was obviously on a fishing expedition for the Nobel Prize. My cowriter, Jan Lövgren, and I stated clearly already in the lede that he was a heavyweight candidate, which may have contributed to the slightly highfalutin tone of the exchange and to our failure to ask any really tough questions. The answers we got were mostly empty clichés. Among other things, we noted that on this occasion he didn't want to criticize Dostoevsky, although on a visit to Sweden a couple of years earlier he had dismissed him as "out-of-date." He glossed over almost everything. Sholokhov, of course, sometimes bellowed out some rather spicy remarks at Soviet writers' congresses, but we heard nothing like that here.

In December 1963 Yevgeny Dolmatovsky paid a visit to the Russian Institute, where he read some of his humdrum patriotic Soviet poetry and answered a few questions. He was quite clearly not in a very good mood. He was shocked to discover that his works stood next to General Denikin's memoirs on the Institute's bookshelf. When he returned home he published an aggressive article in *Literaturnaya gazeta* in which he poked his nose into the private life of one of our émigré teachers. Nils Åke Nilsson sent a sharply worded response to *Expressen*, noting that Dolmatovsky had complained about Sweden before. In a 1957 poem commenting on his trip to Stockholm he had written a poem entitled

"A Nightmare" about a frigid city in which he was aggressively attacked by both buildings and automobiles: "How hard it would be to live here / as a minister (even without portfolio), / as a shrill MP and a soldier in an unjust army."

In March 1964 I strode into the Hotel Foresta in the Stockholm suburb Lidingö and knocked on the door to Ilya Ehrenburg's room. He was here on a regular basis, since he had for some time been having an affair with City Commissioner Hjalmar Mehr's wife. I was interested in his comments on alarm signals about growing anti-Semitism in the Soviet Union—most recently in connection with an inflammatory and disgustingly illustrated book entitled *Judaism without Embellishment*, published in Kiev. Ehrenburg denied that the problem even existed. What else could he do when he was confronted by a total stranger on his own doorstep? But he condescended to speak with me, perhaps because my information (gathered from the émigré press) was of interest to him. I remember him emphasizing that he had talked on the phone with his friend and colleague Leonid Pervomaisky in Kiev just the evening before and that Pervomaisky had not been at all worried. What he didn't mention was that for certain obvious reasons, Pervomaisky chose to hide his Jewish name behind that bold pseudonym, which means "First of May."

In April I served as an interpreter for the exceptionally successful and medal-winning Soviet women's gymnastics team. Two Russians from Kiev who had participated together in previous years stood out from the rest: Larisa Latynina and Polina Astakhova. It turned out that in her room at the same Hotel Foresta Polina was secretly reading a samizdat tracing-paper copy of poems by Osip Mandelstam, who had not yet been rehabilitated or published in the post-Stalinist Soviet Union. It was quite remarkable—an Olympic gold medalist and the Gulag victim Mandelstam, who was still barely mentionable in his homeland. Symptomatically enough, it was thanks to Yulian Oksman, who had passed on the poet's later works to his old friend Gleb Struve at Berkeley, that Mandelstam was rediscovered in the West in the early 1960s.

In Nilsson's advanced seminars I was assigned to present another of the great modernists that were being rediscovered in the West together with the entire "great experiment" in Russian literature and art: Andrei

Bely. It was soon decided that I would write a licentiate thesis on his prose. I had become a Belyist.

In the fall Nikita Khrushchev was deposed, and the Soviet Union entered the long so-called stagnation period. My articles in *Expressen* took the new situation into account. In early 1965 I reviewed two books that had touched me deeply. One was by the satirist Valery Tarsis, who was incarcerated in a mental hospital, and the other was written by General Alexander Gorbatov, whose recollections of Stalin's Terror had been published in the final phase of the Thaw and had now been translated into English.

A passage in my review of Gorbatov's *Years of My Life* indicated the direction of much of my future writing, which arose out of empathy for the prisoners:

> He was taken to the Lubyanka Prison, driven together with other likewise innocent "traitors" and subjected to a series of provocative interrogations. They wanted him to admit he had spied for a foreign power, but despite both physical and mental torture and horrific treatment in three different prisons that sometimes left him unable to leave the interrogation room on his own power, he never admitted any of the charges leveled against him. Later, during his time in the camp, he didn't meet anyone who like himself had managed to avoid signing a confession. Sooner or later the psychological pressure broke everyone, and they admitted to almost anything about themselves and others. This awareness gave him strength in the rare moments when he was filled with despair and was even prepared to welcome death as a liberation.

At one of Nilsson's seminars in April 1965 I talked about Bely's *Petersburg*. This was going to be my topic! Why did this novel affect me so deeply? Because it was a chameleonic text that reverberates with enormous symbolism for Russia. The young Oedipal hero Nikolai Ableukhov is imprisoned – in his room, in his house, in his city. The split in St. Petersburg between the mainland in the grip of the regime and the revolution fomenting on the islands mirrors the rupture in his own psyche. He feels a bomb ticking away in the depths of his being. Russia in 1905 seems to be hanging over an abyss that is at the same time a chasm within himself.

I opened my presentation by pointing out that "Bely's role in the history of Russian literature is difficult to survey and still far from thoroughly explored"—a wonderful understatement, considering what was to come. I applied for a grant from the university to travel to meet Bely's first wife, Asya Turgeneva, who was living among the Anthroposophists in the Swiss village of Dornach. Unfortunately, I was turned down.

Early in the fall of 1965 Andrei Sinyavsky and Yuly Daniel were arrested, accused of publishing "anti-Soviet" literature abroad under a pseudonym. Sinyavsky as a champion of modernist poetry had in particular made fun of Dolmatovsky's empty tirades. On December 5 something remarkable happened. A demonstration in support of the pair was organized in Moscow on Soviet Constitution Day. It signified that a Soviet civil rights movement was slowly taking shape. With the help of the well-informed émigré journal *Posev*, I followed everything closely. I acquainted myself with underground publications such as *Feniks* and *Sfinksy* and read about the SMOG writers who gathered on Mayakovsky Square and about Vladimir Bukovsky, who together with Alexander Yesenin-Volpin was the driving force behind the demonstration, whose demands included something called "glasnost." By this time, I had moved far beyond Yevtushenko—now my focus was on samizdat and the "underground."

December 10, 1965, was a momentous day from a different viewpoint as well. Mikhail Sholokhov was in Stockholm to pick up what became the third Nobel Prize in literature awarded to a Russian. I had attended his press conference a few days before. It was an almost ridiculous performance in which he came off as outright anti-intellectual. He dismissed the earlier Russian laureates as "émigrés"—one external (Bunin), the other internal (Pasternak). They didn't belong in the Soviet Union. He claimed he knew nothing about Iosif Brodsky, who had recently been released and returned from internal exile. He mostly wanted to talk about cows and kolkhozes. Even then voices were already raised wondering whether he had really written the works for which he was awarded the prize.

During these days I worked as an interpreter for a two-man Soviet TV team that had come to Stockholm to report on the celebrated event. What I remember most clearly is how they tried from various angles to photograph the desk in the National Library reading room in which Lenin once sat. It felt bizarre.

In February 1966 Sinyavsky and Daniel were sentenced to seven and five years at hard labor, respectively. The trial aroused considerable attention in Sweden as well, and I carefully read everything about it that I could get my hands on.

Toward the start of June, a group of Soviet writers unexpectedly arrived in Sweden, Bulat Okudzhava and Yevtushenko among them. Soon they appeared in public at a meeting arranged by the radical political association Clarté at the Borgarskolan (the Bourgeois School) in Stockholm. As far as I was concerned, Okudzhava overshadowed Yevtushenko at this point. I managed to attend a party in publisher Per Gedin's home where the Soviet guests met fellow Swedish writers and I could negotiate an interview with him. This was in fact his first trip to a capitalist country, and it would be exciting to get his reactions.

We met for a chat at Hotel Malmen, where the writers were staying. This encounter resulted a few days later in a full-page article in *Expressen* in which Okudzhava spoke as openly as was possible about his problems with the censorship, remarking that what he wrote—it sounded almost like Bely's *Petersburg*—was viewed in some quarters almost as bombs. Despite important differences between them, I drew a parallel with Bob Dylan. Okudzhava himself talked about what Jacques Brel had meant for him. I began like this: "He looks exotic: slightly built, thin and swarthy, with a moustache and black curly hair, a Bulgarian cigarette bobbing in the corner of his mouth. He looks at you with his friendly, rather melancholy eyes. He is 42 years old."

Okudzhava told me that he was working on a screenplay about Pushkin's tumultuous youth in Petersburg and his exile to the south. Much later I learned from Dmitry Bykov's huge biography that that scenario was perhaps one of the best things Okudzhava ever wrote. It never became a film because he had portrayed Pushkin as too provocatively willful and impudent.

Bulat Okudzhava in Stockholm in 1966, with dedication (Courtesy of Jonny Graan)

Yevgeny Yevtushenko in Stockholm in 1966, with a dedication alluding to Okudzhava's "Bud' zdorov, shkolyar!" ("Good Luck, Schoolboy!"): "Bud' zdorov, starik!" ("Good luck, Chap!") (Courtesy of Jonny Graan)

Bykov emphasizes in retrospect that Okudzhava was out of sorts and nervous. Just before his departure he had been warned by ideological instructors about the depraved West, describing in particular Swedish youth groups as full of provocateurs and agents. This was the background to a comical incident that Okudzhava mentioned in our conversation. In front of a Coca-Cola vending machine outside the hotel he had run into what at the time we called a "Mod"—a member of a youth group that on rather vague grounds protested against society. Okudzhava was jittery and feared the situation might turn violent. As it turned out, however, the Mod just wanted to help him wrest that capitalist symbol he had paid for out of the machine.

In my interview he reflected, "We have so many prejudices and wrong ideas about each other. When you actually get a first-hand look you see your preconceptions collapse one after the other. For example, I came here firmly believing that your 'Mods' were depraved, degenerate adolescents. That's completely wrong, isn't it? Many of them are definitely committed politically, socially conscious? Perhaps they are on the contrary the most progressive? There are so many 'legends' going around in the Soviet Union…."

I noted that many of his answers ended in questions: about living conditions in Sweden, about Swedish film, about our churches and our religious services, about how much our cars cost, about the king, about censorship and freedom of the press, about Sinyavsky (whom he'd never read), about Sholokhov's Nobel Prize.

When the article was ready we met again at the hotel. He had me quickly translate my text to assure him that it contained nothing inappropriate. I availed myself of the opportunity to ask on behalf of *Expressen*'s cultural editor whether he would consider occasionally contributing a column. It was a stupid proposal to make in the wake of the Sinyavsky-Daniel affair. He looked a little frightened. His wife confided to me that the recent sentencing of the writers had aroused considerable anxiety among the intelligentsia.

He handed me a collection of his poetry, "The Merry Drummer," in which he had written, alluding to the Latin meaning of my name: "To Magnus—I hope you'll be even greater!" And in the dedication he wrote on

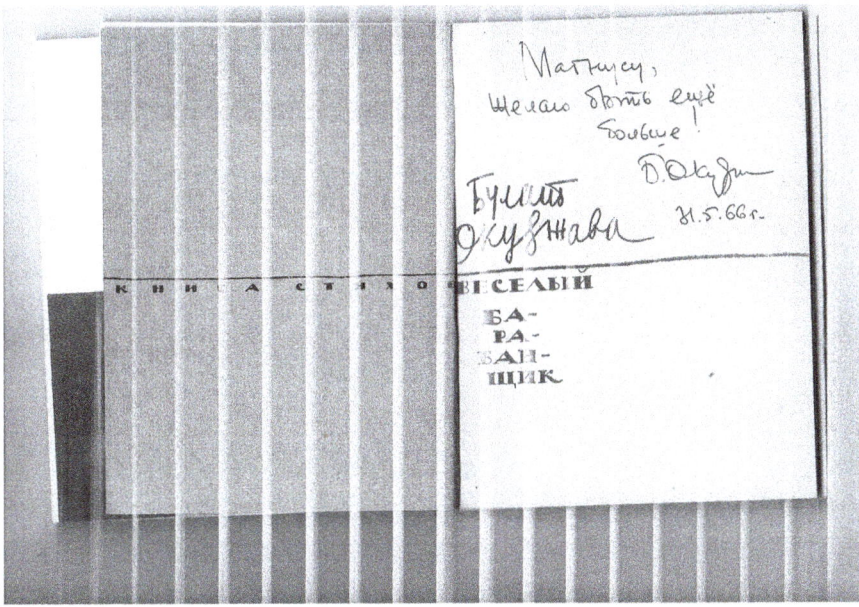

Okudzhava's dedication in "The Merry Drummer"

one of the countless pictures taken at the Borgarskolan meeting he was even more familiar: "Dear Magnus, thank you! I wish you all happiness! Bulat 4.6.1966." We had become friends, it seemed.

Okudzhava was extremely modest. At the Borgarskolan he excused himself by saying that he hadn't played the guitar for three years—which didn't really matter, he added, since he couldn't really play anyway. Yevtushenko, in contrast, was intensely extroverted. When the microphones malfunctioned at this meeting he warned the young socialist organizers that their clumsiness might prove disastrous when they tried to "carry out the revolution." Combined with his declamatory performance, that sort of levity was received well by the audience. At Per Gedin's reception he was in such high spirits that after the writer and comic Hans Alfredson did a hilarious sketch, he planted a spontaneous kiss on Alfredson's lips.

There were two other poets in the background: Robert Rozhdestvensky and Stanislav Kunyaev. They kept pretty quiet. Kunyaev would later show himself to be a nationalist and a harsh and envious critic of both

Yevtushenko and Okudzhava. It was fairly obvious how unpleasant it was for him to be in their shadow. For his part, the result of his visit to Sweden was a poem describing Stockholm as a hostile city full of cold skyscrapers and alienated people: "Alone, like the specter of communism, / I wander across a desolate square." Here there seems to be an echo of Dolmatovsky's confrontation with the Swedish melancholy.

Shortly after this I went to the Soviet Union for the first time. In a writers' house on Lenin Street in Leningrad I paid a special visit to the Symbolist scholar Professor Dmitry Maksimov. He had childhood memories of Andrei Bely. Most important, however, was what he told me about his neighbor Anna Akhmatova, who had died only three months earlier. I had written in *Expressen* about her cautious return to literature and had in fact hoped to meet her.

Maksimov mentioned two significant writers I should get to know: Daniil Kharms and Arseny Tarkovsky. I had never heard of them. In Kharms's case, at least, I redeemed myself. My friend Lars Erik Blomqvist and I soon gave him an unpretentious introduction in our little publication *Rysk bokrevy*.

In February 1967 I finally made it to the Anthroposophists in Dornach, only to learn that I had tarried too long: Asya Turgeneva had died in October. I was dogged by bad luck. Not far from Vevey, where Dostoevsky had worked on *The Idiot* and where I was staying, I went to see Vladimir Nabokov, who was permanently residing in an apartment at the Montreux Palace overlooking Lake Geneva. Completely unannounced, I called him from the reception desk and asked to speak with him about *Petersburg*, which in a 1951 interview with Nina Berberova he had mentioned as a catalyst for all of his own writings. As the case had been with Ehrenburg, it was of course impudent on my part not to have written in advance and set up a meeting. "I don't have the time," Nabokov responded pithily. But at any rate, I got to hear his voice.

In 1968 I defended my licentiate thesis on allusions in *Petersburg*. This was during the so-called '68 revolt. Many in my generation began raving about Mao Zedong and bringing communism to Sweden as well. These born-again Marxists turned out to be insufferable know-it-alls. My experience ran exactly counter to theirs. My commitment was to the Russian civil rights activists. In the fall of 1967 Vladimir Bukovsky had been condemned for demanding freedom of speech and bringing to light the crimes of the past. His only weapon was the pen, but he managed to triumph over his persecutors. He was enormously impressive.

Throughout the spring and summer I of course followed the freedom struggle in Czechoslovakia. On August 21 Soviet tanks rolled over the border. For the first time in my life I marched in a demonstration.

I continued to follow the Soviet civil rights struggle, stage by stage, and soon, in the spring of 1969, I realized that its most important documents, which were often disseminated as samizdat carbon copies needed to be translated into Swedish. So Lars Erik and I compiled what in the fall became a pocket book entitled *Soviet Protest: The New Russian Opposition in Documents*. That spring we also started our little publication *Rysk bokrevy* (Russian Book Review), which dealt with Russian cultural life in a rather cautious Soviet fashion, ignoring trials, arrests, and growing political dissent. This was of course a kind of duplicity. Soon we renamed the journal *Rysk kulturrevy* (Russian Cultural Review).

In the summer of 1969 Lars Erik and I drove his aging Peugeot to Leningrad and Moscow. In many ways that trip shaped us and our interests. The full significance of the meetings we had then was not entirely clear to us at the time, but as it eventually turned out, they held clues pointing toward the collapse of the Soviet state. It was as though we had landed right in the middle of the Russian intelligentsia just at the point in time when that intelligentsia in the narrower sense was about to abandon its last illusions about the Soviet regime. It felt burdened by increasingly heavy remorse after the sentences meted out to Sinyavsky and Daniel and the invasion in Prague, and in the hardening climate of Brezhnev's rule it began to suffer acutely from its isolation. Doors were opened to us everywhere, and because of the stagnant state of things, everyone we looked for seemed to be available. Thus, we were able to get a lot done in a short time, sometimes in a single day. The conversations surged freely, for this was an oral culture in which the hardening oppression seemed to reinforce a genuinely Russian need to talk. The desire to reconnect to a "before"—to a lost, pre-communist avant-garde culture—had by this point become only more desperate.

Myself on Red Square, in 1969 (Photo by Lars Erik Blomqvist)

We learned that the core of the intelligentsia's resistance—especially in Leningrad—had a very strong Jewish component. Intellectuals read samizdat and tamizdat and followed the *Chronicle of Current Events* closely. They conversed in whispers about everything that seemed to be going on beneath the surface, and often continued the exchange on so-called erasable tablets. It almost felt as though we were in a pressure cooker. Several months later, nine Leningrad Jews would attempt to hijack a plane, an act that led to the huge emigration to Israel in the 1970s.

After just a few days we made the acquaintance of a young poet we had read quite a bit about, especially in connection with the trial in 1964 that sent him into exile in northern Russia for his social "parasitism": Iosif Brodsky. The morning we visited him in his little apartment on Liteiny Avenue turned out to be very dramatic. We found him lying on a couch reading the philosophical works of Lev Shestov and the seventeenth-century English poet John Donne. He was on the outermost periphery of society and could be arrested again at any moment. He described the KGB agents shadowing him as "people kleptomaniacs": the minute they saw a free person, their fingers began to itch. Brodsky's friend Yefim Slavinsky (subsequently a familiar voice on BBC's Russian broadcasts) had been detained that very morning. His wife, Tatosha, was suddenly standing there in the apartment in utter despair. What should she do and what was going to happen now? It all seemed like something out of Kafka. Josef K. was lying there on the couch. On the wall hung two posters, gifts from American friends. One said "Wanted: Joseph Brodsky." The other announced a heavyweight boxing match between ruling champion Cassius Clay (as he was then known) and this same Joseph Brodsky. In 1972, as we know, Josef K. was thrown out of the Soviet Union and became Joseph Brodsky for real.

When we left Brodsky's apartment, he went with us. He was constantly looking around him, at every step aware of the KGB men following him. He had been close friends with the excellent young literary scholar Konstantin Azadovsky, but just then they had had a falling-out. When we met Azadovsky, we were struck by the fact that he was even more "backward-looking" than Brodsky, constantly glancing over his shoulder everywhere we went. He was obliged to wait a long time for his arrest.

It didn't happen until 1980, but when it did it was all the more diabolical. The KGB planted a few grams of hashish in his apartment and sent him to a labor camp for three years for "spreading drugs." We strolled around with him in the central areas of the city, which was also one way of eluding the constant threat of being bugged.

One member of the circle we had entered—a Jew, like most of the others—was Yury Mekler, who would eventually become a professor of physics in Israel. He was funny and smart and utterly free of illusions. He saw no hope for improvement in Russia. In retrospect, the scenario he imagined was prophetic. In a situation where Marxist doctrine was atrophying, he anticipated the birth pangs of a Russian patriotic movement. He foresaw at best a future sham democracy with two parties: one communist, the other nationalist. In the end, it wouldn't last anyway, and they would fight together for the good of Russia. It was Mekler who first gave Lars Erik some of the insights that he later presented in his 1972 book, *The Soviet Union Looks Back*.

Eventually, we came into contact with another former political prisoner, Sergei Bernadsky, and his wife. He was not Jewish. Instead, typically enough, he was interested in Russia's lost cultural individuality. In the summer he would take long bicycle tours in the north, where he collected relics of centuries-old Russian peasant culture. Typical as well was the fact that his wife read Vladimir Nabokov in tamizdat and nurtured a cult of her favorite writer. As so many would soon do, she had visited his childhood home in Rozhdestveno, southwest of Leningrad, and tracked down and photographed what remained of the Nabokov estate. Like Mekler, Bernadsky was in close touch with other former prisoners, and together they formed an underground network that naturally played a part in spreading forbidden information. In his kitchen we heard whisperings about the "All-Russian Union for the Liberation of Russia," whose members had been arrested six months previously and been given harsh sentences.

The photographs of Rozhdestveno made such a strong impression on us that we felt that we just had to visit the place. It didn't end well. On the way we were arrested by the police in Oranienbaum and underwent an interrogation that was recorded in detail—in indelible pencil. We had strayed outside the permitted zone. Eventually, we were obliged to sign the report, and I guess we feared the worst. But at that moment our interrogator's attitude changed. We were released with a warning and cordially invited to come again under different circumstances.

Following another line of inquiry, we called on the literary scholar Tamara Khmelnitskaya, one of several older individuals regarded as authorities by young intellectuals. These "mentors" had first-hand experience of avant-garde culture, which, like a sunken Atlantis, was being rediscovered by the younger generation. Khmelnitskaya had written an insightful foreword to the sensational 1966 publication of Andrei Bely's poetry in the Poet's Library series. Since I was now working on a doctoral dissertation on Bely, it went without saying that I should get in touch with her. At one time, she had been one of Yury Tynyanov's favorite students. She had also managed, to the extent it was possible, to preserve a formalist approach to literature. Yet her analytical acumen existed side by side with an aura of innocence, so that in one and the same person we seemed to see before us both a seasoned literary scholar and a young girl. It must have had something to do with her very special background. She had married a young artist at the time of the German invasion in 1941. The day after the wedding, he left for the front and never returned, and from then on she lived her life through literature. In 1946 she was arrested. The guileless young woman understood nothing. Her quiet bewilderment reportedly made even the NKVD waver—perhaps she wasn't really suited to the role of enemy of the people and conspirator. After a while she was released. Now she sat there in a little room in a communal apartment surrounded only by books, a piano, and her husband's drawings.

Khmelnitskaya was able to provide inspired and very interesting glimpses into Bely's archives. Relatively little had been written thus far about him, and no one in the West knew anything at all about such materials. She referred to his then entirely unknown so-called intimate autobiography, in which passages describing Bely's dramatic "other-worldly" experiences in the Dornach colony brought to mind Strindberg's *Occult Diary*. There with her was her friend and classical scholar Yekaterina Melior, once one of Vyacheslav Ivanov's pupils, who began reading aloud for us from a novel she was working on set in fifth-century Rome.

Nina Gagen-Torn and Tamara Khmelnitskaya, in 1974

Suddenly, we were transported from a city in the grip of the KGB to Symbolism, its leaders Bely and Ivanov, and ancient Rome.

From Leningrad we drove via Novgorod to Moscow. There we met a young intellectual we later lost track of by the name of Vladimir Kasaravetsky. Expressing himself categorically, he declared that the entire Russian intelligentsia had given up and given in to the powers that be. The one shining exception was Boris Pasternak, who had met the challenge, passed the test, by refusing to legitimize the death sentences in the Moscow Trials, by persevering with *Doctor Zhivago*, and, finally, by dying a martyr's death. Kasaravetsky was probably not aware of Pasternak's complicated situation in the 1930s. At any rate, he voiced the same sort of pessimism as Mekler. Nothing better was in sight.

At the Mayakovsky Museum we got a few extremely fruitful tips. We were advised to get hold of two persons with a close connection to Mayakovsky: Nikolai Khardzhiev and Viktor Shklovsky. We had already thought of Khardzhiev, especially since Lars Erik had translated his article on Modigliani's portrait of Anna Akhmatova for our first trial issue of

Rysk bokrevy. We came to his home, where we were confronted with his staggering erudition in a shabby little apartment bedecked with priceless canvases by Natalya Goncharova and Kazimir Malevich that he rotated periodically. There was something demonically charismatic about him. He spoke and we listened. He was at times utterly ruthless in his judgments, but his aesthetic sense never failed him. It was obvious that because of his difficulties in the Soviet Union, he was hoping that he might fare better in the West.

We moved on to see Shklovsky, who lived in the writers' quarter. There we were treated to another monologue that was if anything even more worthwhile but somewhat more difficult to follow because of his poor articulation. One of the most fascinating things was that Shklovsky, a cherubic little old man with a bald head and overloaded floor-to-ceiling bookshelves, spoke exactly as he wrote: "making it strange," to use his own famous literary term—phrasing himself very familiarly and laconically, almost aphoristically. He remembered Mayakovsky, Vsevolod Meyerhold, and Sergei Eisenstein, and told us a story about how during the Nazi invasion Eisenstein risked his life to save the executed Meyerhold's archive, which was hidden behind a roof beam in a dacha near Moscow, from the Germans. He tossed off penetrating literary observations almost carelessly. We happened to talk about our own two main interests—Bely's *Petersburg* and Bulgakov's *Master and Margarita*—whereupon Shklovsky pointed out that both novels had been repeatedly revised by their creators and that, strictly speaking, neither work was finished. He found this to be typically Russian, since it also applied to *Eugene Onegin*, *War and Peace*, and *The Brothers Karamazov*. Russian novels are so grandiose that their authors are never entirely satisfied. This was a fresh insight for us.

If the focus had been on Symbolism when we met older intellectuals in Leningrad, it shifted to Cubism and Futurism in our conversations with these Moscow gurus. It seemed only natural to move on to Lili Brik, who just then was out at her dacha in Peredelkino. Because she was Mayakovsky's Jewish mistress, however, his museum held her at armslength and had not recommended her to us. Peredelkino was a little outside the zone open to foreigners around Moscow. We had already gotten into trouble in Oranienbaum and were living dangerously again.

But we risked the short train trip, and we were richly rewarded. We were treated to strawberries that lovely summer afternoon on Lili Brik's veranda in rather illustrious company. Lili's husband, literary scholar Vasily Katanyan, was there, as were Andrei Voznesensky and his wife, children's book writer Zoya Boguslavskaya, theater director Valentin Pluchek, and—last but not least—Maya Plisetskaya and her husband Rodion Shchedrin. Despite Lili Brik's non-official status, it was evident that we were moving in a privileged stratum of the intelligentsia. Plisetskaya and Shchedrin, for example, had arrived in an elegant Citroën. At the same time, however, everyone was noticeably distressed and anxious. Voznesensky sat there and complained morosely about writer's block. When he left the gathering with the remark "I'll go and tap away now" (that is, on the typewriter, in order to finally get something done), someone immediately picked up on the use of "tap" in prison camp slang: "On whom?" Such was the atmosphere, pervaded by an awareness of the KGB's invisible ubiquity.

Maya Plisetskaya had a tremendous presence, charisma. She didn't say much, but you took notice of her immediately. I revealed my naiveté when she and Shchedrin were about to leave in their luxurious Citroën. "Is that your car?" I asked. It was hard to understand how these people who were so critical of Soviet society managed to live so well nevertheless.

Everyone still had vivid memories of the 1920s. Desperately needing to preserve something of her former beauty, Lili Brik suddenly burst out to the tall Lars Erik, "You're standing there now just like Volodya used to." Valentin Pluchek not only recalled the Mayakovsky productions by Meyerhold, to whose troupe he had belonged, but was able with his whole body to give a vivid impression of the way Bely danced around as he lectured on Gogol during a visit to the Meyerhold Theater. At the end of our visit, Pluchek accompanied us to the train. Before we left he vented his sense of shame about what had happened in Prague less than a year before.

In Moscow we went on to visit two friends of Alexander Solzhenitsyn, who was then in disgrace and about to be drummed out of the Writers' Union: Lev Kopelev and Lydia Chukovskaya. Whereas the people we met on the Peredelkino veranda were keeping a low profile and merely kept recalling their guilt over and over, these two stood for civil courage and protest. Both vouched for Solzhenitsyn as a person and a friend. Kopelev had known him since their time together in 1949 in the "sharashka," and it was already common knowledge that he had been the prototype for Rubin in *The First Circle*, which was now being circulated in tamizdat. He made it clear to us that Solzhenitsyn would not at all object to a Nobel Prize—quite the contrary. This was important information. In Kopelev we met an enormously charming personality with warm eyes and a graying Old Testament beard. His apartment was a typical intelligentsia home, only more congenial and cozy. Among the Russian and German literature filling the glass-doored bookshelves there were also photos of friends and intellectual authorities such as Solzhenitsyn, Akhmatova, Mandelstam, Marina Tsvetaeva, and Heinrich Böll. Kopelev had just reread *Eckermann's Conversations with Goethe* although otherwise his specialty was modern German literature. The walls were hung with abstract paintings by artist friends—yet another indication of his non-dogmatic outlook. Vodka was served at a round table—not in the kitchen, for once. One of those sitting beside us now was Kopelev's wife, literary scholar Raisa Orlova. This was obviously an open house in which people came and went almost at will.

Suddenly, right after our conversation about Goethe, a German newspaper correspondent knocked on the door. His name just happened to be Schiller. A friend of the family had a special interest in Sweden, and with her we discussed Lev Tolstoy Jr.'s therapeutic journey to Enköping, which ended in marriage to a Swede. Then another visitor suddenly appeared: Boris Slutsky.

Slutsky had actively participated in the expulsion of Pasternak from the Writers' Union. The guilt he felt over his singular tirades against his Master, the Nobel laureate, (including a rant about Swedish revenge for Poltava) would become a theme in his poetry and, according to several observers, would end up driving him insane. He was noticeably melancholic. Finally, the gathering broke up, and Slutsky served as our very well-informed guide through the writers' quarter, pointing out the residences of hibernating old poets from the Silver Age such as Sergei Bobrov and Ryurik Ivnev.

Lydia Chukovskaya was next on our list. It turned out that she lived on Gorky Street in central Moscow. She contributed new facets to our picture of Solzhenitsyn. Her father, Kornei (who was still alive), had housed Solzhenitsyn in his Peredelkino dacha when he fell into political disgrace and was becoming more and more isolated. She described Solzhenitsyn as an almost perfect creative personality who was at once intensely focused on his work and cheerful and full of joie de vivre. She spoke not a word about her friend's nascent nationalism but portrayed him in all respects as "one of us," a liberal. Perhaps, as Benedikt Sarnov later suggested in his monograph about Solzhenitsyn, she was repressing the truth.

Chukovskaya also vividly portrayed for us her remarkable friendship with Anna Akhmatova, which would soon be given full literary expression in the now classic three-volume edition in which she transforms herself into Akhmatova's own Eckermann. She made it caustically clear that it was Akhmatova who rightfully deserved Sholokhov's Nobel Prize in 1965, and that "Sweden" had caved in to Soviet pressure. Chukovskaya herself was in the spotlight among us that year, since *The Deserted House*, her fictionalized account of Stalin's Terror which had been smuggled out, had just appeared in Swedish translation.

Chukovskaya went on to recall her 1941 evacuation to Chistopol, in Tartarstan, where she'd first met Tsvetaeva. She painted a shocking picture of Tsvetaeva's extreme humiliation just before her suicide: unemployed, barred from publishing, her husband and daughter in prison.

Oddly enough, Chukovskaya did not seem very bothered by the fact that at this point her eyesight was severely impaired. She worked as hard as ever, using tools like thick felt pens. Her walls displayed the usual "icons," of course—Solzhenitsyn and Akhmatova— but also one of Frida Vigdorova, a journalist unknown to us. We later learned that it was Vigdorova who secretly wrote down almost every word of Brodsky's trial in 1964, thereby generating international support for the "parasite."

Finally, there was one meeting in Moscow that was utterly singular yet no less significant than the others. We came into contact with Bely's friend and fellow poet Sergei Solovyov's daughter Olga. She turned out to be a professed Catholic and completely estranged from the surrounding society. There were those who lived as she did during the stagnation period—in small enclaves that preserved ties to the past (her father had by turns been both a Catholic and a Uniate priest before he was arrested and became mentally ill in the GPU's interrogation rooms). How did she make ends meet? With embroidery and seamstress work, by choosing to live at a near-subsistence level. She honored me with an unknown original poem by Bely that he had given to his "brother" the last time they saw each other, in 1931, not long before Solovyov was arrested by the secret police for being a Uniate priest and disappeared into their prisons and mental hospitals.

It was an overwhelming journey brimming with impressions that we needed many years to process. It bore the seeds of the entire Soviet collapse: a dying ideology, an intelligentsia that was slowly taking a stand, Jews on the verge of leaving the country, nationalists in the process of organizing. Solzhenitsyn's resistance struggle, which would result in *The Gulag Archipelago*, the enormous social significance of literature, connections to the past that would grow only stronger. Two Nobel laureates in the making (one of whom we had managed to meet) and a third constantly in the limelight. All of this would culminate in glasnost and then, almost overnight, wipe out the Soviet Union.

When I returned home I found it extremely difficult to describe our experiences to others of my generation. It was a question of two different worlds, after all. In Sweden young people aspired to "build socialism." The Soviet regime hardly even existed here.

The trip resulted in a stream of articles for *Expressen*. This time I concealed my identity behind the pseudonym "Arvid Falk" (after the hero of Strindberg's famous *The Red Room*).

Speaking in a television interview in the fall of 1969, Sivar Arnér, a spokesman for the so-called Swedish third standpoint supported by many left writers, declared that he certainly could understand the sentences meted out to Sinyavsky and Daniel, explaining that the trial showed that literature was taken seriously in the Soviet Union. Two satirists were held accountable for what they wrote—how different from the situation here in tepid Sweden, where challenging the powers that be never had any consequences whatever.

I responded with a polemical article in *Expressen* in which I contended that Arnér's argument was brutal and unreasonable. Just to be on the safe side, I asked him to be more specific. Sinyavsky and Daniel had been sentenced to a total of twelve years of hard labor. Where did he draw the line? How many years in prison were acceptable for daring to criticize? Could he endorse the use of mental hospitals, where certain intellectuals had been committed?

Arnér's response implied that I was an anti-communist agitator incapable of grasping the subtlety in his argument. As a counterbalance, he referred to the little publication *Rysk kulturrevy*, which he said gave a well-informed account of the complex literary life in the Soviet Union. He had just read an exciting mini-essay there about a novel by a certain Mikhail Bulgakov that pointed the way forward for Soviet satire. The ignorant, rancorous Mr. Falk should learn from *Rysk kulturrevy*.

The problem, of course, was that I just happened to be the responsible publisher and one of the two editors of this very same *Rysk kulturrevy*. The article on Bulgakov had been written by my coeditor, the first observer to give a serious presentation of *The Master and Margarita* to the Swedish public. It was all just too comical—Arnér was using me to club me over the head.

Our exchange in *Expressen* prompted the publisher Almqvist & Wiksell to immediately commission Lars Erik Blomqvist to translate Bulgakov. A short while later, *The Master and Margarita*—a cult novel in the making—appeared in Swedish, launching my coeditor's brilliant career as a translator and interpreter of Russian literature.

I was soon immersed in polemics again. Playing on the meaning of the Swedish word "falk" (falcon), the leftist writer Per Olov Enquist expressed his views of my coverage of the Soviet Union in an article entitled "Is Falk a Hawk or a Dove?" My reporting was good, I was informed, but I sometimes made concessions to the émigrés' primitive anti-Sovietism. Evident here as in Arnér's case was a left-wing fear of "émigrés," who were regarded as almost identical with fascists. I retaliated as best I could.

Solzhenitsyn's novels had deeply impressed Bo Strömstedt. In September 1970 he launched a campaign to nominate the writer, who was in dire straits after being expelled from the Writers' Union, for the Nobel Prize. Familiar names were enlisted for the cause: authors Per Wästberg and Lars Gustafsson—and Arvid Falk to boot. Perhaps it helped, for soon Solzhenitsyn was chosen as the 1970 Nobel laureate.

In early 1971 I traveled to Paris to meet some Russian émigrés. I called on a couple of old writers who still had vivid recollections of Bely: Boris Zaitsev and Irina Odoevtseva. Zaitsev was nearly ninety, but his memory was excellent. Restraint and moderation were his hallmark. He gave a clear-cut account of his friendship with Chekhov. He had been a pallbearer at Chekhov's funeral. Six months before that, in January 1904, he had attended the premiere of *The Cherry Orchard*. Chekhov needed to be supported as he tottered into the theater. He told me as though it had all happened just yesterday: "Anton Pavlovich sat in the row behind me. He looked very tired. I realized that he didn't have much time left."

Zaitsev also recounted his early student memories of the future Bolshevik leader Lev Kamenev: he liked to sit backwards on a chair, as though he wished he had a lectern. He described a trip to Italy with future Commissar of Culture Anatoly Lunacharsky, who bummed money from him that was never repaid. He joked about his homosexual colleague Mikhail Kuzmin, who when they had dinner together naturally assumed that Zaitsev would pay, as though they were on a date.

Seventy-year-old Irina Odoevtseva sat there putting on lipstick during my visit. Although she remembered a great deal, it is obvious from her memoirs *On the Banks of the Neva* that she was not as reliable as Zaitsev. As we were chatting, her neighbor at the Russian nursing home in Gagny showed up. It was Yury Terapiano, the author of feature articles in the émigré newspaper *Russkaya mysl*, which I subscribed to and followed closely. Suddenly, he and Odoevtseva began arguing. It seems that, inspired by the Czech student Jan Palach, a young émigré Russian had set fire to himself outside the Soviet Embassy in Paris in protest against communist aggression. Odoevtseva found the deed to be romantically heroic, whereas Terapiano regarded it as simply a manifestation of hysteria. Their dispute ended with Terapiano indignantly slamming the door as he left the room.

In the summer I was once more in the Soviet Union on a short tourist visit. I saw Professor Maksimov again and was able to tell him a little about émigré life in Paris. He was in touch with Bely's bedridden second wife, Klavdiya. I had hoped to call on her, but it turned out to be impossible, for she was not receiving any visitors. Things just didn't work out for me with Bely's widows.

Maksimov and I sat on a bench in the garden at the Academy of Sciences vacation home outside Leningrad. He was extremely tactful. When I happened to misplace the accent on the word "Sarov," St. Seraphim's native village, he whispered the correct pronunciation to me, even though we were alone there. Suddenly he pointed to a window above us and said: "Anichkov lives there. He's Anatole France's son, but it's a secret."

He was cross-eyed, and one eye seemed to stare far away into the sky. He was aware that communism would end someday. But there was one thing he feared: that an eventual collapse would be followed by nihilism, what he called a dangerous "je-m'en-fiche-ism."

In December 1971 a little group of writers including Daniil Granin and Vitaly Syrokomsky, assistant editor of *Literaturnaya gazeta*, came to Sweden. Their first stop was Gothenburg. In a joint article in *Göteborgs-Posten* they stepped forward and complained about the unhealthy Swedish interest in "anti-Soviet" authors. Then they came to Stockholm. I helped as an interpreter. In private, Granin, at least, was radically different. He expressed his admiration for these same "anti-Soviet" writers. "Do you realize how important Solzhenitsyn is?" "Yes, I think we do." "He's rocking the foundations of our entire society." Their stay in Stockholm concluded with a visit to a porn club, to which Syrokomsky insisted on dragging the reluctant Granin. It proved difficult that evening to get him to leave the place. He was quite simply enjoying himself enormously in our capitalist sex swamp.

In January 1972 Vladimir Bukovsky was sentenced to twelve years' imprisonment for compiling a detailed samizdat documentation of the intensified abuse of psychiatry in the Soviet Union. I remember commenting on the verdict in a radio interview. Entitled *Report from the Red House*, these materials were now published in Swedish with a foreword by Lars Erik and me on behalf of Amnesty International. A little while later I went on the offensive in *Expressen* against Carlo Perris, a Swedish professor of psychiatry who had expressed that he could understand the treatment of the courageous "civil-rights general" Pyotr Grigorenko, who had been declared insane and committed to a mental hospital.

In the summer of 1974 I traveled to the Soviet Union by bus with a charter group. As previously in 1969, I purposely sought out writers and intellectuals in Leningrad and Moscow. The Brezhnev stagnation was even deeper. Life seemed to stand still, but things were humming beneath the surface. Solzhenitsyn's showdown with the regime had just climaxed. Around the turn of the year 1973–74 he detonated *The Gulag Archipelago* in the West, and in February he was arrested and deported. That spring he published his essay "Live Not by Lies" in samizdat. At that moment, every Soviet intellectual was forced to define his or her personal relationship with The Lie. Solzhenitsyn was himself living in Zurich and was expected to come to Stockholm in the fall to finally receive his Nobel Prize. His appeal was the obvious topic of conversation in intellectual circles, for *The Gulag Archipelago* had begun to circulate in samizdat.

In Leningrad I visited Nina Gagen-Torn, whom I first met several years earlier. Of Swedish descent, as a young ethnographer she had been captivated by Bely and—as a poet as well—had become his pupil. She had twice landed in a prison camp. The second time, after the war, she was in Kolyma together with Varlam Shalamov. Thanks to her unusual psychic strength and stamina, she was able to provide considerable support for her fellow prisoners. Now retired, she was living with her dog in a communal apartment and just hoping she could get her camp memoirs and poetry published. I squeezed a few verses into the émigré journal *Kontinent* and an ethnographic article in our Slavist organ *Scando-Slavica*, but was unable to find a publisher for her memoirs. Unfortunately, it wasn't until after her death that everything changed, and today she is often regarded as a unique witness to the Gulag. She drew strength from meditative states that in fact originated in what she had learned from Bely and Anthroposophy. On one occasion, she had threatened to bite off the nose of one of her interrogators, which, to put it mildly, was unusual behavior in the cells of the NKVD/NKGB. "I was probably a dog in an earlier incarnation. I only know how to snarl and yelp," she told me.

One evening at Tamara Khmelnitskaya's I met Gagen-Torn and the eccentric poet and translator Sergei Petrov. He got through the Terror

Nina Gagen-Torn with a portrait of her teacher, ethnographer Lev Sternberg behind her, in 1974

with just a year in prison and thirty years' internal exile, far away from the big cities. He seemed to be utterly unconcerned about his Soviet surroundings and also indifferent to Gutenberg's invention. He wrote metaphysical poetry that hadn't an earthly chance of ever being published. He jotted it down with different colored pencils—some poems were red, others blue. Just like Gagen-Torn, Petrov had a special relationship with Sweden. What does that mean? Well, early on he had happened on an 1889 edition of two volumes of the legendary eighteenth-century poet Carl Michael Bellman's works in a bookstore. He was struck by a few lines in *Fredman's 42nd Epistle*: "Close the windows, light a fire in the hearth / as in Kasan / it is cold." Kazan was Petrov's hometown, and that did it—his interest was piqued. He set about learning Swedish passively with the help of dictionaries, and went on in his solitary exile to translate Bellman into Russian. It has been noted that the huge liberties he takes with the original distinguish his subsequently published interpretations from the versions by other Russian translators. The question is whether this may not make him the best of them all, for what he aspires to capture is the essence of Bellman's poetry, not its external form.

The young literary scholar Alexander Lavrov became especially important to me around this time. He had hit on a new manner of writing that was loaded with data, hyperfactual and politically irreproachable yet at the same time free from the least concession to the powers that be. Soon he became my scholarly and stylistic model. He eventually brought his Belyology to a high level of mastery. Somewhat later he and his cowriter Sergei Grechishkin mailed me one of their full-fledged articles, an introduction to Bely's essay "Voloshin's House" in *Zvezda*. A single word had been crossed out: "reactionary," used to describe Bely's Anthroposophy. They did so to draw attention to the fact that this was the censor's contribution to an otherwise entirely objective document.

From Leningrad I made my way out to the writers' summer dachas in Komarovo. It seemed to me that authors tended to become more outspoken among the whispering pines. A group of us sat out on the veranda and chatted. One of those present was Leonid Panteleev, the children's writer who wrote edifying but entertaining books describing how street urchins in the 1920s were re-educated to become Soviet citizens. Now, as he leaned on a cane, he might at first glance have seemed remote from current conflicts, but such was not the case. He turned out to be a passionate early supporter of Solzhenitsyn who had submitted a strongly worded letter of protest against the latter's expulsion from the Writers' Union in 1969. What he told us reinforced our overall impression that many more writers than we realized had shown courage and endorsed Solzhenitsyn's appeal.

In the 1930s Yefim Dobin had been a brutal, "die-hard" critic and literary scholar who ferreted out dangerous ideological and artistic deviations. I learned much later that his derisive sarcasm had driven the original prose writer Leonid Dobychin to suicide. The Dobin I met now was an extremely charming little man who had switched sides and focused his research on Anna Akhmatova. This was a sign of the times. Everything in Brezhnevland was much more complex than it looked on the surface.

Emil Mindlin—snow-white hair and the inquisitive eyes of a child—had a long career as a playwright and prose writer behind him. He had begun in a very exciting circle of poets in Odessa that included noted later writers such as Anatoly Fioletov and Venyamin Babadzhan, both of whom died young. After that, things went well for him. His own writings were not particularly remarkable, but he had a magnificent life story to tell in condensed form in his memoir, *Unusual Interlocutors*, which surprisingly enough had been published a few years previously (and discussed in *Rysk kulturrevy*).

In the 1920s and 1930s Mindlin had been intimately acquainted with almost all the really great writers. He recounted how one late evening in Feodosia, Mandelstam had crawled in through his window and, head held theatrically high, proceeded to fill the entire room with his poetry as he declaimed aloud. Mindlin had been present at the beginning of Mikhail Bulgakov's career in the early 1920s. It was he whom Bulgakov had showered with causeries for *Nakanune*, the journal that served as the future Master's experimental workshop.

Those with whom Mindlin was closest at various times were Marina Tsvetaeva and Andrei Platonov. In 1921, only twenty years old, he had had an affair with Tsvetaeva that resulted in her poetry cycle *The Youth*, which she dedicated to him. In his memoirs Mindlin presented Platonov as a "very, very great writer." He had apparently always known this, before everyone else. He talked about Platonov's intense passion for life and his deep melancholy.

It turned out that Mindlin, too, had a special relationship with Sweden. He had come along as a correspondent when the icebreaker Krasin came to the rescue of the Nobile expedition in 1928. He had helped in the unsuccessful search for the remains of Arctic explorer Finn Malmgren, who had been stranded when the expedition airship crashed, and was later assigned the task of traveling to Stockholm on the return trip from Oslo to inform Malmgren's elderly mother of their fruitless efforts. In Oslo he took the opportunity to become acquainted with Alexandra Kollontai. From a distance, he later wrote about her and followed her career as she rose to an ambassadorship in Sweden. He expressed hopes of being able to return to Stockholm. We soon began to correspond. His daughter was studying Swedish and translated articles in *Rysk kulturrevy* for him. It all looked so promising. His days were numbered, however. He fell ill right at the time I met him in Komarovo, and after that his health steadily declined.

I continued on to Moscow, where I would have new encounters in a somewhat changed atmosphere characterized by a noticeably active struggle for civil rights in which Andrei Sakharov was a prominent figure. First I called on the freethinking communist Lev Kopelev. As became especially obvious when Roy Medvedev, perhaps the last Marxist in the movement, suddenly dropped in, he seemed to be loosening his ideological bonds. Kopelev and Medvedev disagreed about many things, but they got along well nonetheless.

It was Kopelev who had introduced Solzhenitsyn to his friend Heinrich Böll and saw to it that after his deportation Solzhenitsyn was welcomed by his German fellow Nobel laureate. As a result, Kopelev was now living under threat and pressure, and his expulsion from the Writers' Union was sooner or later inevitable. At this moment the civil rights movement was showing serious cracks. On the one side, there was Medvedev's brand of Marxism, on the other, Solzhenitsyn, who even before his exile had written such provocative criticism of the academic intelligentsia that Kopelev's own daughter had repudiated him.

At the moment, Kopelev was most worried about Vladimir Bukovsky, who was reportedly in poor physical condition after several hunger strikes in Vladimir Prison for inmates' rights. Only writers lived in Kopelev's building, including, oddly enough, Bukovsky's own father, a mediocre writer of Siberian rural sketches. Kopelev urged us to support the young civil rights champion any way we could in the West.

When Kopelev heard that I was working on a dissertation on Andrei Bely, he called his colleague Vladimir Piskunov. Before, Piskunov had mostly expatiated on Socialist Realism, but now, like Dobin, he had changed course and exchanged Gorky for Bely. As a result, he was published virtually only in translation—in Ceaușescu's Romania, where he had soon brought out an entire volume of texts by and about the Symbolist. He was also involved in a beautifully designed special issue of a Romanian cultural journal on Bely. None of this was as yet possible in the Soviet Union.

Another new Moscow acquaintance was the translator Tatyana Litvinova, daughter of Stalin's foreign minister Maxim Litvinov. She sat there in a cramped one-room apartment, furnished almost exclusively with books. The civil rights movement consisted of a small group of people who were often related. Together with Larisa Bogoraz, Litvinova's nephew Pavel had led the group of eight who demonstrated on Red Square to protest the invasion of Czechoslovakia and was sent to Siberia for it. He was married to Kopelev's daughter, while Tatyana herself was the widow of Ilya Slonim, the sculptor who had designed Boris Pasternak's original headstone.

Litvinova did not sign protest letters, but she worked underground to support political prisoners. She told me that *The Gulag Archipelago* was an utterly overwhelming reading experience. She had read a carbon copy of the entire work in a single night in order to pass it on quickly to others. She said that it was not until now that she realized the scope of the Soviet regime's crimes. She was also intensely concerned about the fate of Vladimir Bukovsky.

Shortly thereafter, I took the commuter train out to Peredelkino to see Lydia Chukovskaya. In the fall of 1973 she had harbored Solzhenitsyn at her father's dacha. This put her into conflict with the authorities, and finally, at the same time Solzhenitsyn was deported, she was expelled from the Writers' Union. She sniffed contemptuously at the Establishment that attempted in every way to curtail her freedom of movement. Now she was in the midst of a struggle to convert the dacha in Peredelkino into a museum dedicated to her father.

Chukovskaya took me on a tour of the creaking stairways, the walls of which were covered with framed photographs and manuscripts. We sat down in "Solzhenitsyn's room," where I was briefed on the current situation. The Writers' Union was out to take the dacha away from her, but she refused to give an inch: she was a regular tiger. Already at the meeting when they kicked her out she behaved like a victor, declaring that it was only a matter of time before Russia would have its Solzhenitsyn Avenues and Sakharov Squares. (I happened to recall her remark twenty-five years later as I suddenly found myself on the way to the huge Academy of Sciences Library in St. Petersburg—located on Sakharov Square.) She told me that as she stood there and read her statement, the text held very close to her eyes, she had suddenly dropped the pages, which fluttered to the floor and scattered in disarray. None of the old fogeys who had fallen all over each other to censure her could bring themselves to help her, a half-blind old woman. She was forced to pick it all up herself, and I'm sure she did so with dignity. It goes without saying that she eventually won the struggle over the dacha.

General Pyotr Grigorenko had recently been released after five years in isolation at mental hospitals with a diagnosis of "creeping schizophrenia." This was actually a goodwill gesture on the part of the regime in preparation for Richard Nixon's visit to Moscow. I called on Grigorenko on Komsomol Avenue. I was greeted by a vigorous and humble social critic. He told me that his political awareness had evolved in three stages. First came his insight into the real meaning of the Terror in 1937, followed by the discovery during the war that hundreds of thousands of lives had quite simply been pointlessly sacrificed, and finally the realization in the early 1960s that after a few hopeful years of de-Stalinization, the pendulum appeared to be swinging inexorably back again.

Grigorenko stood out as a typical *Homo politicus*. He kept close track of world events during his internment. He talked about the generals in Chile and the colonels in Greece. In the midst of Brezhnev's hardening repression, he declared that he believed in the possibility of a democratic evolution in the Soviet Union. Russians are actually very peaceful, I was told. They have had their fill of violence and bloodshed, so there is no need to fear that dark forces in the soul of the people will be unleashed if the bounds of human liberty are widened.

The spirit of Solzhenitsyn hovered over everything. Grigorenko told me that during their one and only meeting, Solzhenitsyn had urged him to write the true story of "the Great Fatherland War." Grigorenko said that he was not up to such an enormous task, but he did eventually produce a worthwhile memoir that included detailed sections about the war. He was well aware that there was a branch of Amnesty International in Sweden that was working energetically on his behalf.

A few years later, Grigorenko, dressed in an embroidered Ukrainian shirt, would be sitting in a house in Lidingö as a guest of his Swedish

Myself, Pyotr Grigorenko, and Kazimiera Ingdahl, in Lidingö, in 1980

guardian spirits. This was almost at the same time that Bukovsky also paid a visit to the Stockholm suburb. No one could have imagined any of this in 1974. Back then everything seemed so ossified.

Finally, all that remained was an indirect encounter with Bukovsky in Vladimir. We took a bus tour with our charter group to the so-called Golden Ring of cities surrounding Moscow, and when we came to Vladimir a fellow passenger and I made our way to the prison, which we photographed from a hiding place in a nearby stand of trees. Vladimir seemed to encompass the entire Russian paradox. Exquisitely beautiful golden church domes and the infamous prison. We came upon a derelict alcoholic lying in the gutter who knew by heart every poem Sergei Yesenin had ever written. Our bleary-eyed bus driver tossed back a few glasses of vodka and said, "Of course Sakharov and Solzhenitsyn are telling the truth about our society. But what do I need the truth for?"

My final impression was that everything was interwoven with everything else—literature with the civil rights movement and humanist scholarship with the death struggle of Marxism. An inexorable process of ideological dissolution was in full swing.

When I came home, I published an article in *Dagens Nyheter* about Bukovsky, illustrated with the photograph of the prison.

Expressen readily printed my full-page interview with Grigorenko. It was simply amazing, I noted, that he was able to preserve his mental acuity through five years of internment with the mentally ill. Remarkably, while there he had read a copy of *Faust* in the original German, a gift from Kopelev.

In yet another commentary on Human Rights Day—December 10, when Solzhenitsyn picked up his prize in Stockholm—I wrote about the striking contrast between the dreaded Vladimir Prison and the enthusiastic tourists taking in the sights just a short distance away.

Around this time the leading left-wing activists in Sweden announced that the Soviet Union was passé. Now, declared Professor Bo Gustafsson in *Marxistiskt Forum*, an armed Maoist uprising was taking shape there. He had discovered a powerful underground organization in Leningrad "grouped in battalions, regiments, companies and platoons." Well, as for the weapons… I happened to know that he was referring to the nationalistic poets belonging to the "All-Russian Union for the Liberation of Russia," who possessed a rusty old pistol dating from 1898. The KGB had blown things out of proportion, turning the group into a clandestine cell of resistance, and sentenced them to long terms at hard labor.

On one occasion I made so bold as to phone the special clinic for political prisoners in the Ukrainian city of Dnepropetrovsk, where civil rights activist Leonid Plyushch was being held. I asked a doctor some questions and then published the entire conversation in *Dagens Nyheter*. Four months later, Plyushch was allowed to emigrate. It sounds incredible, but it is actually true: shortly after his release he came to Sweden, and there he was one day in our kitchen on Observatoriegatan telling our Amnesty International circle about his martyrdom.

After the 1975 Helsinki Accords, the Soviet Union abruptly embarked on a very limited exchange of political prisoners. Suddenly it was no less a figure than Vladimir Bukovsky's turn. An ordinary Muscovite of extraordinary courage, he was accorded the same status as the imprisoned Chilean communist leader Luis Corvalán. They were exchanged, and Bukovsky, thin as a rail after all his hunger strikes, arrived in Paris directly from Vladimir. It went without saying that I would go to France and view the miracle first-hand, which I did in early 1977. I was unable to meet him personally, but I did attend a "Bukovsky evening" that sufficed for a full-page article in *Expressen* under the rubric "'Which Camp Do You Belong To?' 'The Concentration Camp!'" Bukovsky had burst out of his cell and stood there steadfast as ever and armed as usual with his sense of humor.

While in Paris I took the opportunity to drop in on Viktor Nekrasov, who together with Alexander Galich had organized the Bukovsky evening. We didn't talk about his writing, which had entered a new phase, but chatted instead about Stockholm. After he was driven into exile he had traveled around Scandinavia and was especially charmed by the Swedish capital. He recalled in particular the artwork in the northern line of the subway, which he found unique and worthy of imitation.

One after another they had slipped out of the Soviet Union. Andrei Sinyavsky came to Sweden. Our "Soviet group" within Amnesty International invited him to talk with us. We were told that his seven years in the camps were perhaps the happiest of his life, for they were full of meaning and substance.

In the fall of 1977 I got a one-year grant from the Swedish Institute to do research in Leningrad. Soon I was living in the middle of the city's narrow circle of dissidents. I became acquainted with the historian Arseny Roginsky, who today heads Memorial in Moscow. At his home I met the Red Square demonstrator Larisa Bogoraz, who had returned from exile in Siberia, where for five years she had been forced to cut down trees and haul logs.

My scholarship gave me access to parts of the almost bottomless Symbolist archives. I was able to study the original manuscript of *Petersburg* at the Pushkin House of the Academy of Sciences, a document that Professor Maksimov had rescued from a snowdrift during a wartime bombing attack. It was soiled, and little clods of earth seemed to be stuck to some of the pages. Corrections and deletions meant that there were several layers in the text that needed to be taken into account.

In Leningrad I met with Leonid Dolgopolov, who had just published a book-length collection of articles on *Petersburg*. It marked a beginning. Eventually, some of these materials would be included in the 1981 Russian Classics edition together with Alexander Lavrov's and Sergei Grechishkin's extensive annotations. I supplied Dolgopolov with émigré works edited by Gleb Struve. We got along very well, not least because we both had such an extraordinarily high opinion of Bely's novel. "Bely is the Russian Jung," I ventured to declare on a later occasion. He immediately corrected me: "Not at all. It is Jung who is the Western Bely."

The aged literary scholar Kseniya Muratova did research at the Pushkin House. She had become more and more interested in Symbolism, and in the fall of 1977 she managed to publish a selection of Maksimilian Voloshin's poetry, together with a lengthy foreword, in the so-called little series of the Poet's Library editions. It was a breakthrough. When in the middle of my research trip I went home for a visit, I discovered a pile of these works in the Russian bookstore in Stockholm—it turned out that the coveted volumes were intended only for export. Muratova had not been able to get a single copy of her own. I bought "her" book and gave it to her as a present.

One day in December 1977 I knocked on Marietta Shaginyan's door in Peredelkino. Early on she had played a brief role in Bely's life and had subsequently become deeply involved with his friend and mentor Emilii Medtner. Now, of course, she was a renowned Soviet writer, a much acclaimed Stalin Prize winner. Remarkably enough, she happened to be working on a chapter of her memoirs about none other than Medtner, who interested me more and more as a forgotten key figure in Bely's biography who (after the two had a falling out) ended up as a patient and subsequently as a collaborator of Carl Gustav Jung. She seemed to have nothing against talking about Medtner—on the contrary, she insisted on it. She described him as a "sick," demonically charismatic individual, something with which she had extensive personal experience. Right off the bat she invited me to her ninetieth birthday reception (which I was unable to attend). She told me that the only thing she was afraid of was that Konstantin Simonov, the keynote speaker, would begin kissing her. She didn't like that sort of cuddly silliness.

I had many memorable experiences during my research year. Among other things, I gained admission to the semi-clandestine Anthroposophical commune in Leningrad. One day, a Swedish pastor arrived from the Christian Community, a movement drawing on Rudolf Steiner's teaching, to perform a baptism at the home of one of the Anthroposophists. I served as interpreter—which was easy, since I was familiar with the Symbolists' esoteric language in these rites. When I happened to glance out the window, I was greeted by an enormous neon sign on the roof of the building across the street: "Long Live the Heroic Soviet People!"

One morning in the dormitory I was called down to the hall telephone. I was greeted by a voice on the other end of the line: "Hi, it's Dostoevsky!" For a moment my head was spinning. In this spectral city—in literature, at least—almost anything was possible. Then I remembered that I had recently become acquainted with the great writer's great-grandson Dmitry. He was calling to invite me to a birthday party. He was, in fact, a streetcar driver, but there was a connection to his great-grandfather, for his daily route took him through neighborhoods made famous by Dostoevsky's writings. His little son Alyosha—Dostoevsky's great-great-grandson—wanted to become a cosmonaut.

There were some writers' widows who welcomed visitors. Olga Olesha treated us to toast in Moscow as she offered insights into Yury Olesha's silenced literary career. Under the bed she had a suitcase full of his manuscripts.

Vera Zoshchenko took out old albums and let visitors ponder over the fact that her husband, Mikhail, the great satirist, could never bring himself to smile. She didn't admit anyone until eleven o'clock in the evening. Over a cup of tea, she talked about his heyday in the 1920s, when he was the most widely read writer in the country, and about his humiliation in the 1940s, when he was expelled from the Writers' Union and practically declared a traitor. At that point, I learned, they had both written to Stalin and desperately tried to explain themselves.

Alexandra Fyodorova, the widow of the recently rediscovered and perhaps last custodian of the Petersburg myth Konstantin Vaginov, had herself once been a writer. She greeted visitors in a microscopic apartment she inhabited together with a mentally handicapped son who had been injured shortly after birth during the siege of Leningrad. She had, in a sense, sacrificed her life for him.

I had met Sergei Solovyov's daughter Olga in 1969. Now, during a visit to Moscow, I made the acquaintance of her younger sister Natalya. I got her address from Tatyana Nikolskaya, my colleague in Leningrad who shared my interest in "relics" of the Silver Age. Despite the hell her father had gone through, Natalya had found a place in Soviet society as an instructor at a circus school. She let me leaf through a unique photo album with pictures of her father and confessed to me that in spite of all the difficult and unreasonable aspects of Soviet life, she was not unhappy there. She was allowed to live in peace with her memories in her cluttered one-room apartment. Everything had come to a halt, time seemed to stand still, and that suited her in her old age.

Indeed, I sometimes met elderly people who seemed to be almost happy amid the stagnation. Aleksandr Lavrov introduced me to Viktor Manuilov, who, like Yekaterina Melior—the author of that fifth-century novel—had been one of Symbolist Vyacheslav Ivanov's pupils out in Baku in the early 1920s. Now he was at Pushkin House, where he lived and breathed for his research on Lermontov. He went around in a worn suit and skullcap and with a friendly smile on his face. He was working on an entire encyclopedia devoted to his poet.

In an old building inhabited by a number of writers, I came into contact with Ida Nappelbaum, daughter of the famous photographer. Like Odoevtseva and Fyodorova, she had been one of Nikolai Gumilyov's poetry students around 1920. She showed me pictures no one else had ever seen and told me story after story. In the middle of starving Petrograd, she had hosted a salon for the Russian literary intelligentsia. *Everyone* came, from Yevgeny Zamyatin to Mayakovsky, when he happened to be visiting from Moscow.

Nappelbaum had an unerring eye for the characteristic physical detail. She was able to describe Alexander Blok's crooked, half-insane smile during his final weeks and Anna Akhmatova sitting majestically upright in her chair when everyone else in the circle lay spread out on couches and hassocks. She recounted how, as a precautionary measure, a large portrait of the executed Gumilyov had been removed from her wall

Ida Nappelbaum

and destroyed in the middle of the Terror in 1937, and how she was convicted as a "cosmopolitan" and sent to a Siberian village to cut down timber. She insisted that I convey greetings to her friend Nina Berberova, in the United States, whom she had not seen for over fifty years, and I did so as soon as I came home, which marked the beginning of a new acquaintanceship.

The KGB, of course, kept an eye on my activities. After a while, my Siberian roommate hung a huge portrait of Brezhnev on the wall, which meant that the Soviet leader's face was the first thing I saw when I woke up in the morning. I responded by hanging a somewhat smaller picture of Alexander Blok on my side of the wall.

As I had done earlier, after returning to Sweden I reported to Gleb Struve at the Slavic Department in Berkeley on my impressions. I had gotten to know him through Sergei Rittenberg, who knew everyone in the diaspora and served as an important bridge between the intelligentsia of his former native city of Leningrad and the émigré writers. Struve was grateful for my information and helped me with certain biographical details, sometimes through his childhood memories. We did not touch on the fact that his father, Pyotr, editor-in-chief of *Russkaya mysl*, had once rejected *Petersburg* as "an unbelievably poorly written pile of nonsense." Struve called Leningrad "St. Petersburg," although he added that he was unlikely to live long enough to see the city recover its former name. His prediction came true—he died a few years before it did.

Now, as I was completing my dissertation, I worked for a time at *Expressen*. One day the paper's photographer and I traveled to Uttersberg, a little town some 120 kilometers west of Stockholm, where Ernst Neizvestny—big in every respect— was staying at the home of an art-loving bandy player. Neizvestny, who had a second studio on Grand Street in New York, had miraculously been rescued from the battlefield during WWII. At first, he was in fact believed to be dead. This experience contributed to his enormous passion for life, which I tried to convey in my center spread in the paper. At the moment, he was planning a 150-meter-high sculpture in the form of a human heart that was to represent a greeting from the second millennium to the third. He smiled as he confessed to me, "Jean-Paul Sartre just laughed at my project!" So here was Russian gigantomania linked to an out-of-the-way little village in central Sweden—perfect material for an article.

Big Russia and little Sweden—the theme cropped up again when Vladimir Bukovsky suddenly came ashore and, among other things, called on his old Latvian fellow prisoner Gunars Rode, who had married a Latvian Swede, Ieva, and settled down in a Stockholm suburb. Bukovsky had once saved his life in the Vladimir Prison. Rode was being held in isolation with a life-threatening case of acute intestinal blockage. Bukovsky broke the lock of the cell by ramming a long wooden bench through the door. Then the prisoners began an ear-splitting racket by banging their soup bowls to try to get the prison authorities to react. It worked. At the very last moment, the almost-unconscious Rode was taken to the infirmary. I had them tell the whole story as they posed next to a picture of them together with Rode's wife and newborn twins.

Boris Weil was another well-known political prisoner, with thirteen years in the Gulag behind him. Thanks to Amnesty International, in 1977 he had begun a new life with his family in Copenhagen. Andrei Sakharov and Yelena Bonner had first met in the courtroom in Kaluga where he was sentenced. Now we worked together at Amnesty and also became very good friends. Weil had a wonderfully cheerful temperament that imprisonment had not undermined—on the contrary, his years in the camps became his university. So here was yet another uplifting prison tale. He would soon tell it in his memoirs, and I would review them in *Expressen*.

One day I drove out to call on Lev Tolstoy's Swedish grandson Pavel, who was a landowner in Halmbyboda on the plain near Uppsala. As he strolled around his estate, for a moment he looked like old Count Tolstoy: a well-preserved, vigorous old man. He remembered visiting Yasnaya Polyana as a child, especially the celebration of Tolstoy's seventy-fifth birthday, in 1903. He gave me an interview that also explained why there are so many of Tolstoy's offspring in Sweden. It all started with Lev Jr.'s marriage to the daughter of his Swedish therapist, the famous Dr. Westerlund.

Literary works I reviewed in *Expressen* included Swedish translations of novels by Anatoly Rybakov and Yury Trifonov. Rybakov's *Heavy Sand* is a rich story of a Jewish family, many of whom perished in the Holocaust.

To his own surprise, it got through the censorship. He talked about the book when he visited Stockholm and wrote a friendly dedication in my copy in which he hoped we would continue our acquaintance. I held him to it. As for Trifonov, his *Another Life* afforded revealing glimpses into the hopeless struggle for living space in Brezhnev's Russia. He, too, showed up in Stockholm. There was a deep sadness about him, and he surprised us somewhat when he declared that he probably would have written in exactly the same way had he emigrated. He seemed to be saying that at least on a theoretical level, the thought of exile had occurred to him.

Alexander Zinoviev was another writer with a book on the market. His satirical portrayal of the land of Ibansk in *Yawning Heights* was highly topical. As we chatted over lunch together I was startled by his inflexible oppositional stance. If I put in a single good word about the civil rights struggle, he responded with a surprisingly positive slant on Brezhnev. He seemed to be living with a real dual consciousness. One thing he said stuck with me: "Remember that the frog loves his puddle!" I thought of that when he went back after the collapse of the Soviet Union and became a nostalgic Soviet patriot.

In the spring of 1981 I went to the Soviet Union on a week-long trip that turned out to be chock-full of impressions. I got the opportunity to do an interview with the increasingly besieged *Chronicle of Current Events* and with Ida Milgrom, the mother of long-term prisoner Anatoly Shcharansky, who had been attracting more and more attention of late.

I also called on Marietta Shaginyan. She could praise Stalin and the Polish free trade union movement Solidarity in the same breath. But there was a dab of logic in her reasoning. She wanted to return to the revolutionary zeal of her youth. She had accepted the October Revolution as a Christian phenomenon. Lenin was a Christian without being aware of it. Now in Poland she saw a struggling working class praying to the Mother of God. She was carried away by it.

Her friend Emilii Medtner had consistently belittled Russian "Eastern culture," as represented by peoples such as the Jews and the Armenians, which he felt Germany must discipline. Prey to a neurotic gynophobic syndrome, he had been especially attracted to Jewish and Armenian women. Of Armenian descent, Shaginyan had during the late

Symbolist period become his "little Asian." She responded to this and his entire reactionary attitude by taking a progressive stance in the infamous Beilis trial and turning against what she called "Aryan bestiality." While working on her award-winning book *The Ulyanov Family* in 1965, she secretly discovered that Lenin was one-quarter Jewish, an insight that must have both shocked and appealed to her. As for Stalin, she regarded him as thoroughly representative of something uniquely Caucasian, a brilliant leader who continued Lenin's work and upheld Russia's Slavophile individuality. On top of that was the proud knowledge that both Lenin and Stalin had in fact read her works. Perhaps her Stalinism was ultimately a response to the "Aryan" Medtner's despotic attempt to control and dominate her.

She had a confession or two. When she ran into trouble publishing passages in her memoirs that touched on such topics as her friendship with the banned Symbolist Zinaida Gippius, she jumped in her chauffeured car and drove to the Kremlin, where she negotiated special permission with chief ideologist Mikhail Suslov. But she didn't mince words about the state of the Soviet Union. With his anti-Stalinist revelations, Solzhenitsyn was of course a "bedbug," but Brezhnev was, if anything, even more insignificant, "not worth a button on Stalin's marshal's uniform." In her opinion, everything had indeed stagnated. The working class was "asleep." Brezhnev couldn't even manage to write his own memoirs. She really sniffed at that. She said she knew who the ghost writers were.

Initially, as it turned out, Medtner had consulted Freud before coming to Jung. He had gone to Vienna on the suggestion of his friend, the philosopher Ivan Ilyin, who would soon, in the late spring of 1914, undergo intensive therapy on Freud's couch. Medtner touched on Shaginyan with both Freud and Jung, and on the basis of what they heard from him, both reportedly pointed to a lesbian component in her personality.

Shaginyan's sexuality was assuredly complicated. She revealed to me that once, even as she was exalting Stalin and just after the publication of her much-acclaimed production novel *Hydrocentral*, she had tried psychoanalysis with Ludwig Binswanger in Konstanz (not far from the Jungian Medtner in Zurich) in an attempt to cope with depression and insomnia.

It did not go well, and finally (after a feigned suicide attempt!), she abandoned the effort and fled. Now she explained to me (she had been exceptionally close to her mentally ill artist sister) that incestuous proclivities were something fundamental, of which people had been aware since time immemorial. But when Freud labeled them he made the matter worse. His fateful mistake was that he violated time-honored human taboos, making him "the gravedigger of Western civilization," which was overly rational and therefore spiritually moribund. The wellsprings of life are in Russia, declared this arch-Slavophile.

She gave an example of what she meant. Once, at a film festival in Karlovy Vary, she had a chance to see Ingmar Bergman's *The Silence*. Suddenly, there were some incestuous scenes. She was appalled. Sick to her stomach, she spat as she spontaneously shouted "Scum!" and left the theater.

Like Medtner, Shaginyan had long struggled with hearing problems. Tellingly, she notes in her memoirs that they began in her early teens when she was forced to listen to some girlfriends' erotic confessions. She quite simply tuned out. And that is what seemed to happen to her sex drive as well. She managed nevertheless to have a child, symbolically enough around the time of the revolution and not for nothing with an Armenian.

Shaginyan might have been more than just a kooky old woman with long hairs sprouting from her chin and ears that listened more or less when she felt like letting them. Perhaps there was something of Russia's everlasting contradictions in her glaring paradoxes. Nothing really made sense.

She insisted that I meet Medtner's niece Vera Tarasova, and meet her I did. She had a wonderful trove of letters that the Lenin Library never got hold of, and she gave me unrestricted access to them. She told me I was welcome to come again. I sensed that I would have to apply for another scholarship to return and work both in this private archive and with the Medtner files in the Lenin Library. Plans for a book about him began taking shape.

During this intensive week I also managed to call on two other old acquaintances: Bulat Okudzhava and Viktor Shklovsky. I did a new interview for *Expressen* with Okudzhava in his apartment in "Godless Lane" and also got materials for an article on Shklovsky and his 1923 novel *Zoo*, which had recently appeared in Swedish translation.

Okudzhava in 1981 was not the same person as Okudzhava in 1966. Back then there was an aura of almost innocent curiosity about him. But experience had toughened him, and now he had practically no political illusions. His colleagues were dead or had been silenced or driven to emigrate. He failed to understand how his own people were able to withstand life in Brezhnev's utterly colorless society. All that remained was to bury himself in history in an effort to comprehend the present through the past.

I had meant to present him with a copy of *The Extraordinary Adventures of Secret Agent Shipov*, his tale about the Third Section's early surveillance of Tolstoy, which had recently been translated into Swedish. Unfortunately, however, despite the fact that the book had appeared in several Soviet editions already, it was seized by zealous customs officials and specially summoned security personnel. Why was that? Presumably, it was because of the cover illustration, which showed a cross-eyed, stubble-chinned hero with the nose of a drunkard. Okudzhava said he wasn't surprised.

At the moment, he was in the middle of *The Meeting with Bonaparte*, a powerful novel about the Napoleonic wars. He described how he worked by allowing a number of different plot threads to weave together. He summarized his project as follows: "Each society and each individual carries some responsibility. Sooner or later those who have not taken care of their responsibility will be punished. Someone in my novel points out that Napoleon comes to punish Russia because Russia has been out in Europe for her own selfish purposes."

It is easy to read a topical message in this, I wrote in my article. At the time, in 1981, the Soviet Union appeared to be prepared to march into Poland, and with no other country did Okudzhava have such emotional ties. In Warsaw his songs were for a time if anything more popular than in Moscow. So again: the present mirroring the past.

Okudzhava said explicitly that the voice of conscience, whether of an individual or an entire people, always makes itself heard sooner or later. Just then, he thought the Russian people were beyond hope. He explained that there was something of the slave in the collective Russian psyche—a tendency toward revolt, to be sure, but "never toward freedom."

My article emphasized that in his prose the great troubadour sought out the great junctures in history: the Napoleonic invasion or the emancipation of the serfs in the 1860s. I quoted what he said about conscience, but for his own protection I also censored him slightly by omitting everything about the Russian slave mentality and his inability to understand how people coped.

We were able to help provide Viktor Shklovsky and his wife, Serafima—once married to the repressed poet Vladimir Narbut—with sausage from the special shops and medicine from the West. Shklovsky reciprocated with new stories drawn from his enormous experience. It has been remarked many times how regrettable it is that he never wrote any regular memoirs. Nothing of what he said felt insignificant. He was now eighty-eight years old and very tired, but he still produced his daily ration of writing. He was just finishing *The Energy of Delusion: A Book on Plot.*

Viktor Shklovsky, in 1981 (Photo by Kazimiera Ingdahl)

I called on yet another old writer with roots in the Silver Age: Sergei Shervinsky. His early romance in 1911 with every poet's eternal muse, Maya Kudasheva-Cuvillier came up, which prompted me to look her up later in Paris. In fact, I urged her to write and wish him a happy ninetieth birthday—after seventy years' separation. For a long time now she had cultivated for herself the role of Romain Rolland's widow, and after the two of them visited the Soviet Union under Stalin she was dogged by rumors that she was an NKVD agent. Eventually, she invited me to her own ninetieth birthday celebration. Hoping to score a major interview, I jumped at the chance, but as in the case of Shaginyan's party, it didn't materialize. She passed away shortly before her special day, and instead I wrote an obituary in *Expressen* describing her exceptional role as the lady-friend of Symbolist poets from Voloshin to Konstantin Balmont.

During this trip to Moscow I also met the critic Zoya Kedrina, one of the regime's lackeys who in 1965 had written an infamous article denouncing Sinyavsky and Daniel in *Literaturnaya gazeta* and then served as a prosecution witness at the trial. She happened to be sharing an apartment with Emi Lorentzon, a Swedish woman who had been Alexandra Kollontai's secretary. I interviewed Kedrina, who was still seething with hatred for the two "terrorists." Sinyavsky and Daniel, I was told, had nothing to do with literature. Their works smuggled out to the West were in fact calls for violent revolt. On top of that, they were sex maniacs. "I am a communist," the aging critic exclaimed, shaking her fist. "And I have a party conscience."

Thanks to mutual friends, I was allowed to browse freely in the home library of the still exiled civil rights activist and archival sleuth Gabriel Superfin. There I happened on a copy of *Summer Lightning*, a literary and political anthology compiled by Konstantin Pankeev, the millionaire patron of the arts and father of Freud's patient the "Wolfman," Sergei Pankeev, shortly before the former died, in 1908. The discovery provided new materials for a topic that was beginning to take shape, namely the early breakthrough of psychoanalysis in Russia.

I spent my last evening in Moscow at a little party in the home of another absent prisoner, Igor Guberman, who was serving a five-year sentence in a labor camp. His friend Alexander Parnis had borrowed his apartment and invited a few colleagues. At the time, I knew little about my invisible "host." Soon, I would be influenced by his book on neurologist Vladimir Bekhterev. After the collapse of the Soviet Union, Guberman—with one foot in Israel—would go on to an entirely different career as an entertainer and standup comic.

The literary scholar Leonid Chertkov came to Sweden and spent several days here. Early on, he had served his almost-mandatory sentence of five years in a labor camp. Now he had emigrated to Paris. Living in the world of ideas, he was said to keep books even in his refrigerator. He was impressively erudite. We talked about Kierkegaard and Russia, about the forgotten poet Dmitry Obleukhov, who may have lent his name to the hero of *Petersburg*, and about many other things. It was stimulating throughout, but in the middle of it all Chertkov showed obvious symptoms of mental illness. He warned me about occult radiation that might be emanating from the nearby Soviet Embassy. He thought he saw a face in the wallpaper. He left behind galoshes full of large holes. He has been gone for a long time now, and he has become almost a myth. Papers dealing with him were presented at the big 2010 Congress of the International Council of East European Studies in Stockholm.

One day I did an interview in a café with Alexander Herbstman, an internationally known chess composer who at an advanced age had emigrated to Stockholm during the Jewish exodus of the 1970s. He spoke of his two passions in life: chess and poetry. At the tender age of seventeen, he had debuted in 1917 with a collection of poems entitled *Reflections of Lightning*. Eventually, he studied literature under Valery Bryusov at the Literary Institute in Moscow, where his thesis was a Freudian "Oedipal study" of chess. It seemed that fate had always protected him. He saw friends disappear into the Gulag and asked himself each time why he had been spared. He managed to get on one of the last trains out of Leningrad before the German blockade tightened around the city, and later he fled from Kislovodsk in the Caucasus a day or so before the Nazi troops marched in.

At about the same time, I read Vasily Grossman's novel *Life and Fate*, which had recently been smuggled out. This story about a Jewish nuclear physicist at the center of the mighty national struggle between Stalin and

Hitler made an exceptional impression on me. Providing glimpses of both Lubyanka and Treblinka, Grossman seems to have understood the connection between them before so many others.

In December 1982 I finally defended my dissertation, "The Dream of Rebirth: A Study of Andrej Belyj's Novel *Peterburg*," in which I focused on the profound split in Bely's personality. I showed how he had drilled down into his trauma just as psychoanalysis was experiencing its breakthrough in Russia, and that drawing on echoes of the entire Russian literary tradition, he was able to inscribe his own personal drama into that of the whole nation as it tottered on the brink of world war and revolution. Nikolai Ableukhov is on the verge of bursting, and with him so is Russia. Eventually, the thesis earned me a prize that I accepted from King Carl XVI Gustaf personally.

In the spring of 1983 I was awarded a research grant and spent almost five months in the Soviet Union working at Moscow University. I tried to make the best use of my time to accomplish three basic objectives: conduct research on Russian Symbolism, especially Medtner, in the archives; have conversations with colleagues and also survivors in my area of interest; and finally, make contacts with dissidents and the families of prisoners. During the day, I traveled back in time and immersed myself in the bottomless archives. In the evening, I was often in touch with the core of the intelligentsia and the civil rights movement, which in the course of 1983 was decisively stifled.

Everything seemed to have stagnated. Andropov was so sick that he was never to be seen. The war in Afganistan ground on. Andrei Sakharov and Yelena Bonner were in domestic exile. My friend, Arseny Roginsky was in a camp; another, Konstantin Azadovsky had just been released: he could testify first-hand the bitter cold in Kolyma. The grotesque absurdity of the situation struck me the moment my train crossed the Finnish-Soviet border. I had with me a three-volume Russian-language American edition of Vladimir Vysotsky's songs and poetry about corruption and long lines, about hopelessness and the everyday reality of the prisons. The book was to be a gift from Boris and Lyudmila Weil in Copenhagen to Yelena Bonner. At the time, Vysotsky's gravelly voice resounded across the entire country in homemade magnitizdat tape recordings. Three years after his death, people were still gathering at his grave in the Vagankovo

Cemetery in Moscow. He and his harsh realism lived in the hearts of the people, but nothing was published. The customs officials, of course, immediately pounced on my three volumes. The truth was that they loved Vysotsky as much as everyone else in the country. I was audacious enough to ask them whether they weren't ashamed to steal such a gem to keep for themselves, whereupon something utterly unexpected happened: they gave the books back to me.

I coordinated my research on Medtner between the family archive, where I had a free hand, and the manuscript division of the Lenin Library, where rules and limitations were strict. Medtner was a formidable letter writer. In his correspondence—especially with his wife as soon as they were in different places—he registered his experiences, observations, and idiosyncrasies. This meant that he also reported in detail on his analytical conversations with Jung and provided insights into the psychiatrist's "laboratory"—utterly invaluable materials for anyone who wanted to get a clear idea of his Russian-Swiss bridge building. Some letters were ten or twenty pages long, and often they resembled diary entries. At Vera Tarasova's I was able to read them freely and, with the somewhat reluctant help of the Swedish Embassy, I managed to get hundreds of pages copied. At the Lenin Library I was permitted to order at most three items a day. That was difficult, since a single letter might be an entire item, and there were practically thousands of them. Here there was no way to make copies—everything had to be done by hand. Medtner's relatives allowed me to take anything I thought important. Except for some photos that I could use as illustrations for my planned book, I didn't appropriate anything, in order to avoid breaking up a valuable private archive.

I had now also become interested in Medtner's psychoanalytical guide Ivan Ilyin. In the manuscript division at Moscow University, I studied the then Menshevik's diary from the revolutionary autumn of 1905. I was amused to note that I was listed in the visitors' register as "Lohengrin." With the assistance of a future minister in Boris Yeltsin's government, the friendly art scholar Aleksei Komech, I made my way out to Ilyin's family plot in the Novodevichy Cemetery. I also found distant relatives of his who showed me photo albums from which, unfortunately, all pictures had been ripped out during the Terror. At that time, Ilyin was a fierce anti-Bolshevik and monarchist with whom it was dangerous to have anything at all to do.

Freud may have given this Russian maximalist with violent personality traits insights into something fundamentally infantile in his psyche, but he certainly did not cure him. In his relationship to Russia he remained, as Ilyin himself put it, a child in its mother's lap.

When I returned to Sweden I called Anna Freud in London to ask her how many Russian patients her father treated. She replied in a frail voice, "Two or three." That tallied with my conjectures: Pankeev, Ilyin, and, for one week, Medtner.

Everything in this Land of Andropov was built on paradoxes. Nothing was really clear-cut. The ideology had been undermined to such an extent that the regime was forced to look for support to Symbolism and Alexander Blok, who in connection with the recent centennial of his birth had been heralded as a great patriotic poet. My university advisor had switched from Gorky to Bely. Although Chingiz Aitmatov's latest novel *The Day Lasts More Than a Hundred Years* drew on an old Kyrgyz myth about the *mankurts*—prisoners whose heads had been wrapped in camel skin that shrunk and tightened as it dried until they lost their memory—it was awarded a state prize. The Soviet Union was living in a kind of *mankurt* reality, but oppositional voices percolated through nevertheless. When I wasn't buried in the archives I was given access to a reading room for professors in which there was a copy of a physics journal featuring Andrei Sakharov's latest scholarly article, even though its author had practically been declared an enemy of the people.

One day I was invited by the Institute for Slavic and Baltic Studies to lecture on Medtner and the early Russian interest in psychoanalysis. This was a unique free zone, headed by the two encyclopedically erudite scholars Vyacheslav Ivanov and Vladimir Toporov. Soon both of them welcomed me to their homes.

Ivanov especially wanted to inquire about current psychoanalytical theories in the West. His interest had to do with the fact that young people in the Soviet Union (some of whom lost themselves in occult speculations while others became alienated Oblomovian figures) had such obvious personal issues that there was a crying need for new psychodynamic ideas.

The dinner guests at Ivanov's included a young female psychologist and the psychiatrist Viktor Gindilis and his wife (who was of Swedish descent). Gindilis was a fascinating acquaintance, since he had roots in both medicine and the civil rights struggle. He was Jewish and had grown up while his father was in the Gulag. He gave us an inside account of the political mental hospitals and described how the diagnosis of "creeping schizophrenia" that was often applied to dissidents had arisen at the infamous Serbsky Clinic. Eventually, our conversation touched on Sabina Spielrein. Ever since her letters and diaries had been discovered a few years earlier in a Geneva basement, worldwide interest in this key figure in the early history of psychoanalysis, the Russian link between Freud and Jung, had grown considerably. I had made up my mind to get in touch with any surviving relatives in the Soviet Union to try to shed some light on her fate. The prevalent opinion in the West was that she had perished in Stalin's Terror. Now I learned that there was a biochemist in Moscow by the name of Menikha Spielrein and that she was evidently the daughter of Sabina's brother Isaak, a professor of psychotechnology.

Ivanov wrapped up the evening with something quite remarkable. He brought a little blackboard and chalk to the dinner table and began to lecture as he sketched on the board. His topic concerned whether a high-tech civilization might have existed in Africa around the time of Christ's birth that later collapsed and disappeared without a trace.

Ivanov had been the famous psychologist Alexander Luria's secretary in his final years, and now he guided me to Luria's daughter Yelena. What interested me was Alexander Luria's psychoanalytical circle in Kazan in the early 1920s. Yelena, a biologist herself, allowed me to look at the family archive. It contained the minutes from meetings of the Kazan group, as well as a letter in Gothic script from Freud himself. As we delved into the past, Yelena began reflecting on her father's earlier marriage and told me about his first wife, who was still alive and probably knew more. So she spontaneously picked up the phone and called her. They had obviously not had any contact with each other for decades. It was an emotional conversation: tears streamed down Yelena's cheeks so profusely that she could barely speak. Suddenly I realized how absurd it was that a stranger like me should be sitting there, involved in complex family relations.

I had a telephone conversation with Militsa Nechkina. A prominent historian and expert on the Decembrist revolt, she had also been a member of the Kazan circle. I almost felt like an archeologist when I reminded her of something that seemed to lie hidden in her past, namely her psychoanalytical interpretations of literature as sublimation and other things.

She had ignored all this for decades.

The walls in Toporov's apartment were all covered in books. He seemed extremely preoccupied, his gaze fixed on something far off in the distance. Referring to my lecture, he noted that in the early twentieth century, the Russians were always in the vanguard, so of course they were also the first to adopt the new therapeutic ideas of the times. Subsequently, everything just went into decline. He regarded the communist epoch as an awful national cataclysm. At present, the country was in a seemingly endless decadent phase. "But just remember one thing," he added. "Sooner or later, Russian literature always overcomes power. In the long run, it is invincible." And he gave me an example: in 1937, at the height of the Terror, Stalin was forced to turn to Pushkin for legitimacy. The centennial of the national poet's birth was celebrated in parallel with the slaughter.

According to Toporov, only ten or fifteen people in all of Russia had any insight into the real state of society. Oddly enough, in the Lenin Library I found exactly the same words in Andrei Bely's memoirs in unpublished passages commenting on the situation in Russia during the years that particularly interested me: 1913–14. In retrospect, I sometimes think that I and everyone else half-consciously used the past as a kind of filter in our attempts to understand what was going on around us in the present. The crash came very soon, in fact, just as it had back then. Things were not as petrified as they seemed. Only eighteen months later, Gorbachev came to power, and soon, under glasnost, the forbidden literature would burst in like a shockwave.

I eventually found Menikha Spielrein living in a dreary concrete suburb called Tyoply Stan. Suddenly there I was on her doorstep, describing to her in a single breath the nascent world fame of her aunt. She had difficulty connecting this information to her memory of an aunt whom she, as a young member of the Komsomol, had regarded as impractical and out of step with the times, almost helpless in everyday Soviet life.

She could only stammer three words: "S uma soiti!" ("It's enough to drive you crazy!")

I soon learned that Sabina—utterly disillusioned with communism, under which her three brothers, all of them working in different scientific fields, had been executed—had trusted the Germans' reassurances and refused to flee from Hitler's troops when they occupied her native city of Rostov. Ultimately, she and her two daughters and hundreds of other Jews were shot in the so-called Snake Ravine outside the town. Stalin and Hitler had quite simply divided up the family between them.

Menikha recalled her father's arrest in 1935. She was nineteen at the time. As a pioneer in psychotechnology, he was especially close to Sabina. Menikha loved him above all else in life, yet at the same time she had been brought up as a Soviet person, full of enthusiasm for the building of the new society. She couldn't make rational sense of the dreadful events. Her father's disappearance and her mother's subsequent internal exile remained a mystery. It was as if the family had been shattered by a force of nature. Shunned by her peers, she was forced to leave the Komsomol.

Menikha Spielrein, in 1995

Then along came Khrushchev's de-Stalinization, and once again her father's name could be spoken aloud. Nobel laureate Igor Tamm himself delivered an oration to the memory of her physicist uncle Jan, and Professor of Psychology Solomon Gellerstein paid a warm tribute to her father, Isaak. She and her mother sat there in the first row and listened. The horrible wound was torn open, and she cried and cried as twenty-five years of repressed anguish poured forth.

In later years, Menikha devoted more and more of her energy to the memory of Sabina, translating her texts and participating in conferences. Born in Berlin during WWI, her name means "peace" in Hebrew. Her lifelong dream was to see Berlin once again. When, at more than eighty years of age, she finally got there, she suffered a stroke that led to her death.

After returning to Sweden I published an article in *Expressen* about my meeting with Menikha that included the new information about the deaths of Sabina and her brothers and the first known photographs of her. It turned out that shortly before, in the *New York Review of Books*, the famous psychologist Bruno Bettelheim had sent out a call for information about her relatives. In his memoirs, he eventually tried to take a bit of the credit for the scoop, implying that it was he who had sent me on the mission. That was not true.

Soon a lecturer came to the university from a state research institute to drone on about Poland's unfortunate situation. Interest was minimal: out of a student body of thousands, all of eight people showed up to listen. She declared Poland to be "the center of the international class struggle." Solidarity was mentioned only in passing as "the underground provocateurs," and she expressed apprehensions about the pope's forthcoming summer visit to Poland, which she characterized as a scheme devised by the class enemy and directed in secret by the CIA in collusion with the Vatican to provoke new "social explosions." The interesting thing was that her portrayal of the Polish church was a perfect description of the Soviet Communist Party: a massive propaganda machine that forced the citizenry into subjugation, young people apathetically performing empty rituals, an utterly diluted and moribund faith. Afterward, a visiting Irish student asked, "How is it that I've never met a single Polish communist?"

The lecturer answered, "That just goes to show how serious the situation is. Polish society as a whole needs to undergo some rigorous training in Leninism."

After her lecture she probably went home and complained like everyone else about the wretched state of things, perhaps while listening to Vysotsky on her tape recorder. Was she schizophrenic? No, she was simply equipped with a Soviet double consciousness.

At the Gorky Institute of World Literature, I met the erudite Byzantologist Sergei Averintsev. A few years before, he had aroused attention with a knowledgeable and perfectly non-Marxist article in the extensive *Encyclopedia of Philosophy* about Sophia, the Divine Wisdom. We discussed Jung, another subject of which Averintsev had an excellent grasp. As for the double consciousness, he interpreted it almost psychoanalytically as a trait of pretty much every Soviet citizen.

Early one morning I called on art historian and literary scholar Ilya Silberstein. He was well advanced in age and suffered from diabetes, but he still worked like a horse. He received visitors at seven o'clock sharp. It was he who long ago (in 1932) had started the excellent scholarly series *Literaturnoe nasledstvo*. At the moment, he was immersed in a huge five-volume edition of materials relating to Alexander Blok and Symbolism that would become volume 92 of the series. He seemed completely unaffected by the opposition he constantly faced. He could imagine including Bely as well in the publication. Priceless art hung on his walls. On one occasion when he had landed in serious political difficulties, he traipsed over to the Central Committee and quieted the muttering at the price of "one Aivazovsky." Silberstein was born to succeed. His position was not exactly weakened by the fact that he had also been married for some time to the head of the Central Archive for Literature and Art.

I called regularly on Nikolai Khardzhiev, whom we had first met back in 1969. He actually acted in three roles—literary scholar, art expert, and collector—and he was equally prominent in all of them. If his writing was always obsessively precise and factographic, in his personal relationships he was instead temperamental and intense. It was uncanny how he had managed to rescue a cultural treasure. He had collected modernist art and literary documents—drafts, manuscripts, letters—and saved them from destruction when they were all anathema. Denunciations and terror had no effect on him. Throughout the entire Soviet period, he remained steadfastly loyal to his mission, guided only by his infallible aesthetic sensibility. Along the way, he surely must have had to make various political concessions, but if so, they were worth it.

As soon as a visitor got settled, he would begin to generously share his memories in a kind of one-man theatrical performance. He had been present everywhere and known almost everyone, except for Khlebnikov, whom he ranked first among the poets, and Mayakovsky, about whom he had written the most. The poets and artists had in their turn held him in high regard. On one occasion, Anna Akhmatova complained that although he understood her poetry better than anyone else, he had not embraced it with genuine love. Osip Mandelstam spoke with admiration of his absolute pitch. Daniil Kharms appealed to his "genius," urging him to begin writing prose of his own. The person who had meant the most to him was Malevich, who like a father or brother had helped shape him by intervening at an early stage in his maturation process. Later, during WWII, Khardzhiev had repaid his huge debt of gratitude by saving the manuscript of Malevich's memoirs from the fire that a group of shivering people had lit in the painter's library to warm themselves.

For a time, Khardzhiev had shared an apartment with Kharms. In the fantastic gallery of characters he portrayed, it was in fact Kharms who had amazed him the most: "I never really understood how he managed even to cross the street without getting hurt."

He had plans to emigrate to Sweden with the help of a Swedish friend and, using some of his priceless works of art to provide the financial backing, begin publishing. The project had ended in collapse and bitterness. Now he wanted me to help him try again. I declined, however. Perhaps I was wrong.

There in her tiny studio apartment stuffed full of books sat Marina Tsvetaeva's eighty-eight-year-old sister and colleague, Anastasia, a survivor of eighteen years of labor camps, tough and utterly free from illusions. "There's a lot of talk in our society about progress," she said. "But in fact the twentieth century was a regression. Things are going backward." She warned me, an inveterate newspaper reader, against reading the daily press. She had done so, I was told, on only three occasions in her life: the first time about Tolstoy's death; the second—for some reason—when General Kornilov attempted a political coup in the summer of 1917; and the third time when Eleanor Roosevelt visited the camps and the Gulag authorities invited the prisoners to read about her trip through their Potemkin village.

Anastasia had just published her memoirs in the form of a 650-page doorstopper that told about growing up in symbiosis with her brilliant sister. Their fates were forever interwoven. Both suffered at the hands of the Soviet regime. When Marina decided to take her own life in 1941, Anastasia was already in the Gulag. But for Anastasia, she had never really died, for the two sisters had spiritualistic meetings to the very last. They would meet on the crowded streets of Moscow, and Marina regularly left signs and signals "from the other side." These occult fantasies were all the more remarkable coming from Anastasia, who was otherwise so clear and precise in everything. When she talked about herself, she was at the same time speaking about Marina. Perhaps we can say that Marina did not finally die until 1993, together with her then ninety-nine-year-old sister.

I learned more about Andrei Sakharov's peculiar life in exile at the home of mathematician Yury Shikhanovich, who was a close friend of Yelena Bonner. Since 1980, he had been one of the secret editors of the *Chronicle of Current Events*, while "officially" he wrote articles for the popular mathematical journal *Kvant*. The *Chronicle* was still being disseminated in typewritten copies, reporting on all that was unseen in Soviet reality: arrests and trials, new samizdat literature, and current conditions in the camps. It was an absolutely essential source of information.

Shikhanovich looked rather frail, but he was tough. He knew what he had taken on. One evening he held party to celebrate his fiftieth birthday, where despite the serious situation, activists gathered in good cheer. Yuly Daniel's son Alexander (now one of the driving forces behind Memorial) was there, as were the excellent balladeer Pyotr Starchik; Leonid Vul, who was a former editor of the *Chronicle* and the grandson of one of the executed camp commandants of the 1930s ("As long as I have my Vul, I'm safe," Stalin used to say, before his henchman's luck changed); theater scholar Yury Eichenwald; disability rights activist Yury Kiselyov; and others.

I happened to end up sitting between Eichenwald and Kiselyov, who had the same first names and patronymics. I was told that this position gave me the right to make a wish, so I wished that we could finally learn what happened to Raoul Wallenberg. Kiselyov, who had no legs and rolled around on a wheeled board, was the maximalist of the group. Looking me straight in the eye he said, "Any Swede on Russian soil who doesn't constantly try to find out about Wallenberg has betrayed his duty."

Shikhanovich, Starchik, and Eichenwald had something in common: at various times they had all been interned in psychiatric hospitals for their political views. Eichenwald had been declared mentally ill as early as 1952. There at the clinic, he had jotted down Gorky's bombastic poem *The Song of the Stormy Petrel* on a scrap of paper. The doctor who was treating him took this socialist classic to be a manifestation of his mental illness. The attitude toward him reportedly did not become any kinder once the mistake was discovered. Despite the fact that he had published his satirical study *Don Quixote on Russian Soil* in the West, for some time now he had not been visited by the KGB, not even for the lightest search of his home. He interpreted this neglect as a deliberate strategy on the part of

Yury Kiselyov, Yury Eichenwald, and myself at Yury Shikhanovich's fiftieth birthday party
(Photo by Alexander Daniel)

the security service: to ignore everything and pretend to pay no attention, and then suddenly strike.

One evening, "Shikh" invited me to a performance of Ionesco's *Rhinosceros* at a little basement theater in the suburbs. The absurdist play seemed to mirror the deceptive conformism of stagnant Soviet society—a uniformity that was something quite different beneath the surface. My Danish roommate at Moscow University told me how amazed he was to see an artist praise the party on TV one evening, only to meet him the next evening in a private setting and hear him warn Denmark against socialism. That's how it was.

Through "Shikh" I became acquainted with his fellow mathematician Vadim Yankov's wife, Natalya Sarmakesheva. Her husband's research in the field of hyperintentional logic had gradually tilted more and more toward moral philosophy. Shortly before the military takeover in Poland in 1981, he had sent out a seven-page samizdat letter in which he urged the Soviet working class to follow Solidarity's example in order to 1) regain self-respect, 2) recreate a sense of social inclusion, and 3) demonstrate nonviolence as a means to restore personal freedom. In January 1983 he was sentenced to seven years' imprisonment and internal exile for those seven A4 sheets of paper. At the time, he was still in pretrial detention at the Lefortovo Prison. I interviewed Natalya, who was left to care for their three children in the Moscow suburb of Dolgoprudny about the high price the family had had to pay for his exceptional courage. She answered tersely: "To be able to stand tall at least once in your life and tell it like it is—that's worth seven years."

Natalya was allowed to send Vadim two one-kilogram packages of food per year to supplement his meager prison rations. She and I went to a special Beryozka store bursting with luxury goods that was off-limits to ordinary citizens and bought sausage and chocolate. She also got a bottle of wine for herself. On their wedding anniversary, she grabbed the bottle and took a symbolic turn around Lefortovo, after which she went home and ceremoniously drank it.

Around a crowded and abundantly laid table of *zakuski* in Larisa Bogoraz's apartment I had a chance to meet her amiably reserved ex-husband, Yuly Daniel. She was at that time married to Anatoly Marchenko, whose death three years later from the effects of a hunger strike would open the way for Gorbachev's mass release of political prisoners. It was as

Bulat Okudzhava, 1981. Photo by Kazimiera Ingdahl

Vadim Yankov, Natalya Sarmakesheva, and their daughter Anastasia

Natalya Sarmakesheva flanked by her daughter Anastasia and her son Ilya

though being a prisoner's wife was her profession in life. Her only weapon was the Remington typewriter with which she wrote a constant stream of letters and appeals to the authorities demanding logic and consistency of the dictatorship. She was indefatigable. What was it that drove her? "I feel so sorry for Russia," she replied. It was as simple as that.

During my stay in Moscow I made a little side trip to Leningrad, where among others I called on the imprisoned Arseny Roginsky's wife, Natalya Frumkina, and their little son, Boris. Together we went to the children's theater in Leningrad's Pioneer Palace to see a Russian dramatization of the Swedish author Jan Ekholm's book about the fox cub Ludvig. Enormously popular in the Soviet Union, it had appeared in Russian translation in 1974, shortly after Solzhenitsyn's "Live Not by Lies" appeal. Rather remarkably, Ekholm's text seemed to echo Solzhenitsyn's. The hero is little Ludvig, who has been raised by his large family to cheat and swindle. He turns out to be utterly incapable of lying, however, which has consequences for the entire panic-stricken species. The auditorium was packed with perhaps more parents than children. The atmosphere was tense, and some lines in the play were greeted with stormy applause.

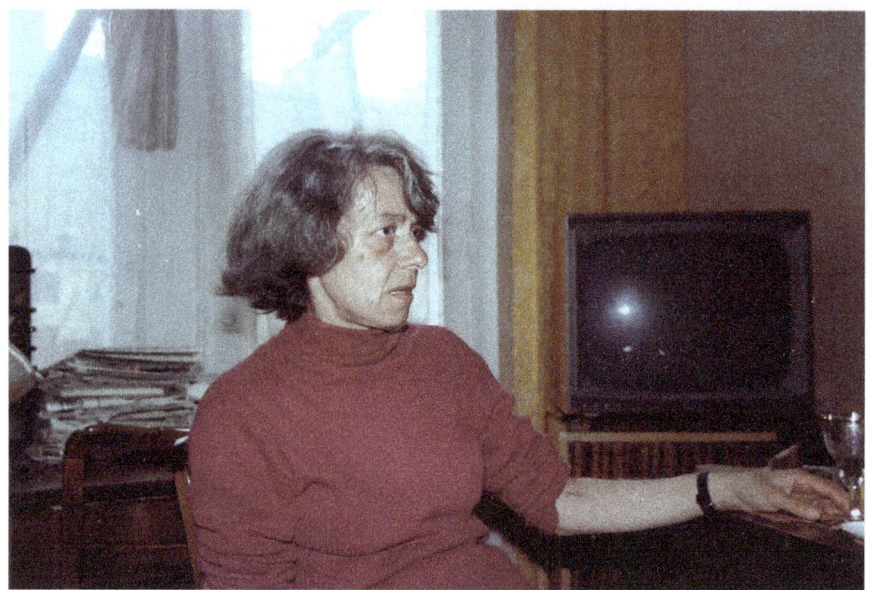

Larisa Bogoraz (Photo by Kazimiera Ingdahl)

At Tamara Khmelnitskaya's I met one of Russia's best poets: Alexander Kushner. Professor Maksimov had remarked on this pupil of his in our conversations seventeen years earlier. We discussed psychoanalysis in particular. Kushner thought that great men such as Freud and Jung were totally unable to anticipate and understand the mechanisms of totalitarianism and their effect on the psyche. I was forced to agree with him.

Soon, literary scholar Mikhail Meilakh arrived in Moscow, accompanied by his colleague Georgy Levinton, an old acquaintance of mine who also lived on the vulnerable periphery of society. Meilakh now published annotated editions of works of the OBERIU group in the West. He told me he could feel how the KGB was slowly tightening the noose around his neck. I treated the pair to lunch at the unlikely Hotel International, which had been hastily knocked together by the Soviet Union's favorite multimillionaire capitalist, Armand Hammer, in the middle of the old working-class district Krasnaya Presnya. The brand-new building housed seven upscale restaurants, three saunas, a specialty food store, a perfume store, and a Beryozka bookstore.

Shortly after I returned home I received word that Meilakh had been arrested. He was later sentenced to two years in a labor camp and five years of internal exile. Shikhanovich was arrested in the fall and also got seven years, which forced the *Chronicle* to cease publication. A fifteen-year epoch was over.

People, people, and more people. I must concur with Russian iconologist Engelina Smirnova, another member of the circles in which I moved during these intense months. She and her colleague Gerold Vzdornov helped me get in touch with even more people who still remembered the Silver Age and generously invited me to social gatherings in their homes. Engelina told me—and she meant it in a friendly way—that I didn't care much about physical details. People and their fates—this was and is what mainly interests me.

In early 1984 I got a letter from none other than Nina Berberova. Since 1978, I had been serving as a messenger between her and Ida Nappelbaum in Leningrad. Berberova was also my colleague now, since she had ended up as a professor of Slavic studies at Princeton. I had sent her my dissertation, which she enthusiastically welcomed. She addressed me as "one of our most prominent and subtle authorities on Boris Nikolaevich," adding that she would very much like to meet me and reveal (she loved her little secrets) some rather sensational details about this Boris Nikolaevich Bugaev, aka Andrei Bely. She stressed that the meeting would not only be between Slavists but would also take place "on a more personal level." She simply wanted to give a more intimate account of what she knew about Bely's traumas and to tell about her own personal experience of the inhibitions and fortunate sublimations that she regarded as a legacy of the sex-hostile age that had shaped both her and Bely.

She said that she had read my book "with enormous interest" and was impressed by my "enormous knowledge" of Bely's life and works. She stressed that she had known him well, but that he was interested in her only in her role as the wife of Vladislav Khodasevich, who in the early 1920s was his best friend.

She was quite remarkably open. She imagined that Bely, like all intellectuals born between 1860 and 1900, had "held his nose" at the mere mention of Sigmund Freud's name. She noted that she was a member of a sexually inhibited generation who between the ages of three and fourteen were doused "every evening" with ice-cold water to forestall "forbidden dreams"; thereby young girls were deprived of "their sex" and rendered cripples. She had read Otto Weininger when she was fourteen and realized that (with his interpretation of the individual as a bisexual being, we must assume) he had transfigured her "for her entire life." Zinaida Gippius had similarly "worshipped" Weininger, but Freud disgusted her. Berberova and Khodasevich had read Freud in the late 1920s, but he hesitated to admit it openly out of fear he would be boycotted.

In August 1984 I returned to Moscow. This time, I called on Armenian-born Zarui Apetyan at the Composers' House on Gorky Street. By a remarkable coincidence, Natalya Sarmakesheva, Vadim Yankov's wife, worked as a concierge in the same building, and from there she supplied me with current information about prisoners in the camps scribbled on tiny scraps of paper, which I in turn smuggled out, hidden in my socks and later forwarded to Amnesty in London. Apetyan was a prominent musical scholar who was well acquainted with the Medtner family archives, but she was also very frightened. She was the widow of composer Gavriil Popov, who had been harassed and persecuted in the Stalinist campaigns of the late 1940s. There she sat, a few stories above the temporarily employed wife of a prisoner, and loudly praised the Soviet Union's new leader Konstantin Chernenko, who was so old and weak he could barely stand.

On a village street in Peredelkino I ran into a major Soviet writer: Valentin Kataev. I saw my chance. Lydia Chukovskaya had once described this dacha neighbor of hers to me, saying that "he was born a bad person." The amazing thing, however, was that in the autumn of his years, this "bad person," with so many betrayals behind him, redeemed himself as an artist with a kaleidoscopic mosaic of memories, especially from the Odessa of his youth. Kazimiera Ingdahl had just defended her dissertation in Stockholm on his fellow Odessite Yury Olesha's *Envy* based on her archival research in Moscow, and I spontaneously thrust a copy of her thesis into Kataev's hand. I wanted to tell him something about her work, but at that very moment there was a cloudburst that forced the umbrella-less Kataev to run for shelter. It was a little disappointing, for I would never see him again.

At an intersection there in Peredelkino I chanced the same day to bump into Yevgeny Yevtushenko. I recalled our 1966 meeting in Stockholm and mentioned that I was on my way to see Anatoly Rybakov. Yevtushenko took the opportunity to praise Rybakov's novel *The Children of the Arbat*, which he had just read in samizdat. When I arrived at my host's dacha and told him about this, he was delighted. It was just what he wanted to hear about his silenced text. He sat there intently following the Olympic boxing matches from Los Angeles on TV. He was a real fighter himself, and far from floored.

It was even more difficult than before to describe my experiences to Swedish acquaintances. They couldn't understand the stifling atmosphere in which Soviet people were living. Gunars Rode remarked at an informal Amnesty meeting that the Soviet system was going to fall apart at any moment. Now, of course, we were the ones who didn't follow. Was he serious? Just like that, overnight? Unless you had been locked up in Vladimir for years, it was quite simply impossible to sense how close it was. In just another six months, Gorbachev would become general secretary of the Communist Party.

In the early fall of 1984 I traveled to Bergamo to attend the first international Bely congress, organized by the elderly but very energetic Georgian Ukrainian Nina Kauchcisvili. Balmy evenings on the piazza in the late summer warmth of the hilly northern Italian city were a perfect backdrop for this historic event. Leonid Dolgopolov and Alexander Lavrov were sorely missed in the Soviet delegation, but otherwise there was a broad spectrum of participants, and Kauchcisvili's cheerful temperament and the twinkle in her eye kept spirits high. Bely scholarship appeared to be entering a new phase. In the United States there was already a regularly published bulletin with news "from the front."

I reported in *Expressen* on poet Irina Ratushinskaya, who fought in the women's zone of the political camps for prisoners' rights with constant hunger strikes that put her in solitary confinement. She had been sentenced to twelve years' hard labor and internal exile: "The harassment continued in the punitive cell. Ratushinskaya responded by starting an open-ended hunger strike to protest the brutality of the guards. She demanded in particular that the cell be heated—the temperature was around 9–12 degrees Celsius [48–53 °F]." For twenty years now I had been providing detailed accounts of conditions in the Soviet prisons and the ordeals suffered by the inmates.

In May 1986 I made a quick visit to London, and during two busy days did a one-on-one interview with Janko Lavrin, who had recently turned ninety-nine. It was my Moscow colleague Alexander Parnis, who has done a superb job of digging up every trace Velimir Khlebnikov has left behind, who induced me to get in touch with Lavrin, with whom he was in letter contact. Perhaps it occurred to him that I often sought out elderly individuals with a broad experience of life. Lavrin had come to St. Petersburg from his native Slovenia in 1907. As an active Pan-Slavist, he collaborated with none other than Vladimir Bekhterev. In 1910 he received a greeting from Lev Tolstoy via their mutual friend Tomáš Masaryk. He was personally acquainted with Symbolists and Futurists, especially Khlebnikov, whom for a time he had lodged in his apartment and given free access to his South Slavic library. During WWI he had served as the Balkan correspondent for the conservative newspaper *Novoe vremya*. There he was in reality playing a not entirely attractive double role, however, since he was at the same time allied with the Futurists' most extreme faction, a group calling itself "The Bloodless Murder," which proclaimed "the aesthetics of the insignificant." His young friends soon poked holes in this dual role of his. Ilya Zdanevich wrote a satirical absurdist opera about "Janko's" adventures in the Balkans. Surrounded today by a legendry aura, it was written in Khlebnikov's so-called transrational idiom and has been described as one of the most radical linguistic experiments ever undertaken in Russian.

After emigrating to England in 1917, Lavrin soon allied himself with the enigmatic Alfred Richard Orage's journal *The New Age*, where he introduced Dostoevsky to English readers from a psychoanalytical perspective. Eventually, he became Professor of Slavic Studies in Nottingham and wrote on the history of Russian literature. He seemed to remember all of the remarkable events he had witnessed in his early years, although he sometimes had difficulty giving exact dates. The interview resulted in an article in *Expressen* and materials for future essays, especially the one that appeared in a Russian anthology of articles dedicated to Lavrin published twenty-five years later.

Soon something startling happened. In the midst of the incipient new Thaw, I was paradoxically declared persona non grata in the Soviet Union. The KGB had caught up to me. The news came as a shock. Actually, of course, it all could have happened much earlier.

In the autumn of 1986 the exiled Taganka Theater director Yury Lyubimov visited Stockholm. He produced *The Master and Margarita* and a potpourri of Pushkin's "little tragedies" at the Royal Dramatic Theater. One evening he treated us to a one-man show at Lars Erik Blomqvist's that provided some rich insights into his long Soviet career. What he described over dinner was a sheer Absurdistan. I especially recall his comments on the brilliant satirist Nikolai Erdman's enlistment—after his return from Siberian exile—in the NKVD's song-and-dance ensemble and his description of Vysotsky as a self-immolating genius who in fact lived seven lives simultaneously and therefore truly was old when he passed away at the age of forty-two.

Now I had to turn toward other points of the compass. In the late winter of 1987 I attended a conference on Russian literature and psychoanalysis in summery California, where I delivered a paper on the breakthrough of Freudianism in Moscow, St. Petersburg, and Odessa during the years prior to WWI. One half of the audience consisted of Slavists, the other of practicing psychoanalysts. Suddenly the whole subject had become a hot topic.

On the way, I stopped off in New York and Washington, D.C. In New York, I called on Zinaida Grigorenko, who had recently lost her husband. She lamented the fact that the Perestroika Gorbachev was proposing had yet to have any effect whatever on the situation of the political prisoners. The broad amnesty came the following year. Andrei Sakharov and Yelena Bonner were allowed to return to Moscow from exile in Gorky. It was a huge relief. Something big was in the offing.

In Washington I was able to survey documents pertaining to Medtner in the so-called Rachmaninoff Collection in the manuscript archive at the Library of Congress. Medtner's correspondence while in emigration

Janko Lavrin, in 1986

revealed him to be a full-blooded fascist: Bely's supporter ultimately came to pin all his hopes on Adolf Hitler. It was Nina Berberova who had alerted me to this gold mine, about which she herself had only a vague hunch. Now the idea was that we would get together at her home in Philadelphia. Unfortunately, however, she caught a cold and the meeting didn't take place, so instead we spoke over the phone.

Two elderly Russian writers—Marietta Shaginyan and Nina Berberova—had given me invaluable help by tipping me off about two fantastic archives. A Stalinist and an American professor might seem to be poles apart, but they had points in common. In 1921 they had first met at Blok's funeral, which was a historical watershed. They were both of Armenian descent, both were to some extent musicologists, and both lived to a ripe old age, each with her own unique experience of the turbulent twentieth century. Berberova was able to return to the Soviet Union in 1989. By that time, Shaginyan had long been dead, but she and Nappelbaum saw each other again for the first time in sixty-seven years. The remarkable reunion was immortalized on television in Leningrad.

I was still banned from the Soviet Union and was forced for the time being to be content with the company of Russians in Sweden. In the fall of 1987 I met Yuliana Yakhnina at a translators' conference. Besides being a veteran translator of French literature, she had for a long time already been rendering an enormous cultural service to Sweden through her excellent, sensitive translations of our great writers. In reality, she was a niece of the Menshevik leader Yuly Martov, Lenin's old colleague, who later opposed him and was thrown out of the country when he protested against both the October coup and the mass killing that followed. Born in 1928, just as Stalin came to power, Yuliana had been named after her uncle, in a covert political allusion on the part of her parents. With the help of a pocket dictionary, in the 1950s she had begun translating from Swedish, and Swedish literature became her second home, a haven from the brutal regime that had nearly wiped out her entire family.

Yakhnina seemed to know the entire Russian intelligentsia, and we lost ourselves in endless conversations. On her mother's side, like her uncle before he assumed his nom de guerre, she was a Zederbaum. Her relatives had suffered greatly as early as the 1920s. In 1945 an American journalist asked Lavrenty Beriya about the Zederbaums. "There are none in Russia," Beriya responded. But Yuliana and her mother had survived.

Tsvetaeva's biographer Irma Kudrova paid a visit to Stockholm from Leningrad, bringing with her greetings from my old colleague Dolgopolov and a book, a new version of his anthology of articles on *Petersburg*, with a generous dedication: "To my dear friend Magnus Ljunggren, who in this book will find reflections of his own theory." He meant that he had been influenced by my dissertation.

Another visitor from Leningrad was philologist and poet Vladimir Admoni. Over lunch at home with us he gave a poignant account of how the Stalinist anti-cosmopolitan campaigns had physically, if not psychologically, broken his wife and colleague Tamara Silman. Admoni had belonged to the circle around Akhmatova, who was of sterner stuff than she. "Don't worry," she had told Admoni in 1944 as she prepared to return to Leningrad from evacuation in Tashkent. "I'm a tank."

In the summer of 1989 we traveled to Switzerland, a surrogate for Russia. I sought out places connected with Medtner and called on his distant relatives. We also visited Dornach, where all the Russians who had known Bely were now gone. And we followed in the footsteps of Bely and Medtner's friend Ellis (Lev Kobylyansky). Ellis epitomized and made Symbolist duality his hallmark, and he influenced Bely's *Petersburg* far more than was realized. He had passed the final quarter of his life in a villa in Locarno-Monti with an incredible view of Lake Maggiore. The creative peace he knew there differed starkly from his rootless nocturnal escapades in Moscow during the heyday of Symbolism. In reality, however, there was a link between the two periods. In exile he channeled his dualistic outlook into an effort to synthesize Eastern and Western culture. It seems that he traveled the same path as Sergei Solovyov and in the end became Catholic-Orthodox.

In Russia, glasnost had now reached its apogee. It was an ecstatic time for literature. Now and again I published lively little news items on developments in *Dagens Nyheter*.

In the fall of 1989 Larisa Bogoraz and her fellow civil rights activist Vyacheslav Bakhmin paid an official visit to Sweden to study the Swedish correctional system. When visiting the Österåker Prison, she was nearly dumbfounded to discover that it was not walled in. She joked that in Russia, some sort of external barrier was necessary, mostly to keep people out of such desirable "sanatoriums."

Yuliana Yakhnina returned to Sweden, accompanied by writer Sergei Kaledin and his wife, who was related to Yuliana through their common Polish ancestry. A likeably modest young man, Kaledin's work had recently been translated into Swedish. According to the title of the anthology he handed us, it was a collection of "bad plays." In reality, his critical and revealing texts were quite promising, but eventually he withdrew to the countryside and little more was heard of him.

I was almost isolated from the world myself. My life revolved around the Symbolists as I worked intensely on my book about Medtner, which was nearing completion.

In 1990, after five years of banishment, I was once again granted a Soviet visa. I had managed to upgrade myself to a member of a writers' delegation participating in the big centennial celebration of Pasternak's birth. There I sat at the Bolshoi Theater in the company of Raisa Gorbacheva; some members of the Central Committee; Adam Michnik, the symbol of the Polish intellectual resistance; Lars Erik Blomqvist; Solzhenitsyn's Swedish translator, Hans Björkegren; Yevtushenko; Bernardo Bertolucci; Arthur Miller (who was so tall that he blocked poor Nils Åke Nilsson's view, and many others. On stage, Andrei Voznesensky recited Pasternak's poetry.

Now the persecuted poet was portrayed, even in huge posters, as a crucified martyr who seemed to symbolize the fate of all Russia on the Golgotha of the twentieth century. The audience included Gorbachev's most outspoken opponent in the Politbureau: Yegor Ligachev. He looked rather subdued. I went up to him and asked him for an autograph. He readily complied, and we struck up a conversation. Who was I? I let slip that I wrote a thing or two about Russian culture in *Svenska Dagbladet* (to which I had recently been invited to contribute an article). At that moment, the Politbureau reactionary asked me to say hello to the readers of the conservative Moderate Party newspaper. It was crazy: here was the last, recently ostracized, guardian of Bolshevism sending his best to our bourgeoisie.

The next day we gathered in a huge demonstration at Pasternak's grave in Peredelkino. Yevtushenko gave a speech and recited poetry.

Just under a year later, in June 1991, only a few weeks before the attempted coup that would lead to the collapse of the Soviet Union, I went to Moscow again for a medical congress. My neurosurgeon brother, Bengt, invited me along to serve as his interpreter.

Everything seemed to be pulsating. It was difficult to find physical food in the shops, but there was spiritual nourishment aplenty. Bookstores overflowed with previously forbidden literature. I was forced to buy a sizable backpack to carry all the books I'd bring back to Sweden.

My brother and I began in Leningrad because we had published a joint article on Vladimir Bekhterev, the courageous neurologist who had consistently challenged the tsarist regime but ultimately—or so it seems—was done in by Stalin. In 1927 he had been called to the Kremlin to examine the rising dictator's arm, which had suddenly become stiff. Fearless as ever, Bekhterev is said to have diagnosed the complaint as a case of hysterical paranoia. The next night he died under unclear circumstances, possibly from poison. Was he perhaps one of Stalin's first victims?

We had sent our article to Bekhterev's granddaughter Natalya, who at the time was the foremost Soviet neurologist, and she invited us to meet with her. We were picked up at the hotel by her private chauffeur and taken out to the holiday homes of the Academy of Sciences on the Gulf of Finland. She treated us to a glass of wine and agreed to chat about her family. Her father was shot in 1937. She confirmed that her grandfather really had been ordered to the Kremlin and that he had made some sort of provocative diagnosis. Beyond that, nothing could be said for sure about how he had died. On that point she demanded proof and documentation. And we concurred. There were already enough Soviet urban legends going around as it was.

What shocked us was that Bekhtereva was at the same time open to the occult currents that were becoming more and more prominent as society collapsed. A charlatan by the name of Anatoly Kashpirovsky was running rampant on TV, claiming that he could heal people as they watched him on the screen. Bekhtereva said she was interested in his "supernatural" powers. With support from Gorbachev, she had just opened the Institute for the Human Brain in Leningrad, where she had installed measuring instruments to register Kashpirovsky's "bio-field." My brother was almost speechless. Perhaps we should take into consideration the fact that for seventy years everything had been explicable and subordinated to a rigorously materialistic world view. Now that outlook was cracking, and even prominent neurologists were beginning to waver.

After visiting Bekhtereva, we went to the Psychoneurological Institute founded by her grandfather. When we asked our special guide in the museum section there whether it was certain that Bekheterev had been done away with, we were told that a couple of Swedish researchers had in fact recently proved that he was. The guide happened to be referring to us.

In downtown Leningrad I took the opportunity to call on the city's most legendary dissident, Ernst Orlovsky, who, symbolically enough, resided near Uprising Square. For decades he had tirelessly acted as though the Soviet Union were ruled by reason, issuing letters and protests based on his enormous legal expertise demanding consistency and logic. Yet he had in fact not spent a single night in a KGB jail. An omnivorous consumer of everything from Yevtushenko's poetry to Ukrainian statistical yearbooks, there he sat now amid a sea of books and newspapers penning new sharply worded appeals to various authorities. It almost seemed as though he were in the process of winning a war of attrition with the increasingly mangled Soviet regime.

Our fellow travelers in the charter group suddenly turned out to be mostly Swedish Ingrians who had come to celebrate Midsummer—St. John's Eve—on a country hillside in their former domains. We met up with them and were treated to something very special, as thousands of Ingrians from all over the world—Soviet Estonia, Sweden, Finland, Germany, and Canada—gathered together to mark the resurrection of the nation after the long Soviet ice age with singing, dancing, folk costumes, and eating and drinking.

It was also a snapshot of the current situation, in which stifled and oppressed national cultures were moving toward rehabilitation.

We continued on to Moscow, which sweltered under the summer heat. While my brother listened to presentations at his congress, I called on Yakhnina. Now, in the midst of the social crisis, it was a golden age for entertaining whodunits. She acknowledged that she had begun to be interested in Frank Heller, a Swedish pioneer in the genre whose works are often set in a cosmopolitan milieu.

My brother had just read Professor of Pathology Yakov Rapoport's account of how, in connection with the infamous Doctors' Plot in early 1953, he had landed on death row in Lefortovo Prison, where he remained until the entire affair was dropped after Stalin died. This was the Bekhterev case in reverse: a number of prominent Jewish doctors were accused of attempting to poison the tyrant, whose relationship with physicians had always been full of drama.

Rapoport published his book during glasnost, and it was quickly translated into English. Now it turned out—so small is the circle of the Russian intelligentsia—that Rapoport was Yakhnina's second cousin. She had no trouble in arranging a meeting with the ninety-three-year-old former death row inmate.

Rapoport was a warm-hearted white-haired man who hadn't lost his passion for life and still had a child-like inquisitive glint in his eyes. He had recently married a woman in her early seventies. The couple lived on the eighth floor of a high-rise with no elevator, but the old man bounded up the stairs with ease. What he described for us was a Dostoevskian experience. Like the great writer, who was "pardoned" minutes before a mock execution, a quirk of fate had given him a new lease on life. The nightly interrogations at Lefortovo, where he was accused of being a terrorist, had been utterly horrible, and he actually experienced a feeling of security each time he was brought back to his cell, which under the circumstances was in any case his own little patch of territory.

I took the train out to Peredelkino and looked up yet another pair of formidable survivors. Lev Razgon was over eighty years old but well

Yakov Rapoport, myself, and Yakhnina in 1991

preserved, as old camp inmates were sometimes. He had once belonged to the communist aristocracy. His first wife was the daughter of Gleb Boky, a high-ranking functionary in the party and the secret police. In 1937 he was arrested and shot, and when he disappeared, his daughter and son-in-law also vanished into the gloom of the Gulag. Razgon's wife perished, but he survived eighteen years in captivity. In the camp he met his future second wife, the daughter of a leader of the Socialist Revolutionary Party. The two of them were moved often and were frequently physically quite distant from each other, but they miraculously managed to keep in touch through the barbed wire. In the 1960s and 1970s, Razgon became a noted writer of popular books on Soviet science, but he remained silent about the Gulag until he published his memoirs during glasnost.

I was especially struck by the fact that Razgon was already talking about communism in the past tense. Like Rapoport, he had an indomitable faith in life that nothing had been able to shake. The year before, he had for the first time traveled abroad in connection with the publication of his book in France. Now he declared that in the long term and for her own sake, Russia must bring communism to trial and at least symbolically prosecute any guilty parties who were still alive. He was not seeking revenge but merely wanted the courts to pass judgement on the monstrous crimes that had been committed.

Yevgeniya Taratuta, the other victim of Stalin I visited, had an even more shocking tale to tell. What this seemingly gentle babushka revealed about her past was in such glaring contrast with the resplendent summer idyll all around us. She had grown up in a Russian anarchist family in Paris. Her father was a disciple of Prince Kropotkin, and she remembered Emma Goldman visiting them at home. In May 1917 she and her parents were repatriated. Her father never became a Bolshevik, but he accepted Leninism as a lesser evil than capitalism. She herself eventually found refuge as a children's writer.

In 1937 Taratuta's father was arrested and shot. She was spared. The real blow came much later, in 1950, when Stalin's anti-cosmopolitan campaign reached its climax. She was arrested because she was Jewish (and moreover had an anarchist past) and was locked up, first in the

Yuliana Yakhnina, Lev Razgon, and Yevgeniya Taratuta in Peredelkino, in 1991

Butyrka Prison and then in the Lubyanka. Her interrogator demanded that she admit she was working for the intelligence services of three different Western countries. One of her tormentors in particular beat her in the face, on her breasts, and on her back. To avoid breaking down and losing her mind, as she was being abused she began rattling off to herself poems by Pushkin and Mayakovsky. It helped.

In 1951 Taratuta landed in a labor camp above the Arctic Circle amid fifteen hundred disabled women with numbers on their backs, all of them torture victims. They were not given any work to do. Survival depended on being able to withstand temperatures approaching 60 below zero. I noted that her fingers looked like windswept tree branches, the result of being forced to peel potatoes that were so cold that her hands froze. Some Ukrainian peasant women finally freed her from this task in return for reciting the plots of familiar literary works for them. For a second time, she was saved by the Word.

The art of survival in various forms. Elderly people with unbelievable tales to tell. Small remaining pockets of social democratic, socialist revolutionary, and anarchist resistance. Literary critic Lyudmila Saraskina once wrote that Russian TV made a terrible mistake in the 1990s when it neglected to document to a greater extent the life stories of this gradually dying generation. She is probably right. During these few days, we certainly gained some insights. So many tales still needed to be told.

Close to the White House is Rochdale Street, named for a nineteenth-century English weaving cooperative. I was there once again, poring over old letters and manuscripts in the Medtner family archive. A wasp stubbornly buzzed around the room. Less than two months later, the whole picture would change, with Boris Yeltsin standing up on a tank outside the Duma and crowds pouring out into the streets to protest against the putschists and the state of emergency.

I later wrote in *Dagens Nyheter* about Taratuta and her resistance, which I interpreted as representative of the entire people's rebellion against an inhuman social order built on lies and crimes. The continued existence of the Soviet Union was by that point a question of months.

Unlike several of my fellow Slavists, I had never done any translating, but now I began working on Yelena Bonner's autobiography, *Mothers and*

Daughters. Just then it seemed particularly urgent. It told about the Great Terror, how her beloved stepfather was arrested and shot, how her mother was interned for eighteen years, and about how the privileged party milieu in which she had grown up was completely ravaged. Her experiences must have profoundly influenced Sakharov's political engagement. Eventually, information leaked out about how the Central Committee had discussed his dependence on this "evil Zionist." Her memoirs appeared just a few months after the collapse of communism. I stressed in the foreword that *Mothers and Daughters* could well be read as encapsulating the fate of the nation: "This book tells us something very essential about the rise and fall of the Soviet Union, about its appalling mass murder, and about how people ultimately rose up and beheaded the Hydra."

For a brief, dizzying moment, it looked as if Russia were moving toward a new freedom. But that was not to be.

When my biography of Medtner was almost completed, in the summer of 1993, I traveled once again to Switzerland to meet Franz Jung, a charming eighty-five-year-old architect who greeted me in the library of his father's enormous house overlooking Lake Zurich. He was able to identify every single person in the group photographs of Medtner and the Jungians that I had brought with me from the family archive in Moscow. He was in some of them himself. Suddenly he exclaimed, "How extraordinary that a Swede should come along and ask me about what happened in my life seventy years ago!" In Russia, something like that was, of course, quite natural, for 1921 and 1922—the years we were talking about—were so much closer there that seventy-year-old events seemed to have happened just yesterday.

After several articles describing the rampant anti-Semitism of certain Russian literary nationalists such as Alexander Dugin and Alexander Prokhanov—a phenomenon that had become typical of the current state of unrest and disintegration—I was summoned to testify as an expert in a Swedish parliamentary hearing on the situation of the Jews. I pointed to a dangerous fascist tendency in post-Soviet Russia, a trend that I would follow closely in later years.

My monograph *The Russian Mephisto: A Study of the Life and Work of Emilii Medtner* finally appeared in 1994. It presents a detailed portrait of a forgotten but once prominent figure in the turbulent intellectual atmosphere that reigned during the Symbolist period. By all indications, Medtner conveyed something important from Bely to Jung, both of whom had from their respective standpoints warned about the gap between the intellect and the psyche and between the conscious and unconscious that threatened to split the modern individual unless the two spheres were linked by the strongly anchored structure that Jung calls the Self and which Bely symbolizes in the bridge that joins the mainland and the islands in the schizoid "personality" of his city.

In the fall of 1995 I traveled to Moscow together with director Elisabeth Márton's film team, which was making a documentary on Sabina Spielrein. I helped Márton get in touch with eyewitnesses who still remembered her. Above all, of course, they included Menikha, who by then was devoting all her time to her increasingly famous aunt. But there was also Vladimir Schmidt, for example, the son of polar researcher Otto Schmidt and his Freudian psychoanalyst wife, Vera. There in art patron Stepan Ryabushinsky's remarkable art-nouveau mansion, which had once housed the Psychoanalytical Orphanage-Laboratory and later Maksim Gorky, Vladimir Schmidt recalled how things were back in the early 1920s, when he himself was living there.

In 1996 I got a lectureship in Russian language and literature at the University of Gothenburg and became a long-distance commuter. The following year I went to Moscow, where among other things I delivered a lecture at the Russian University of the Humanities, which has its own center of Swedish studies. It was a fantastic time of freedom and debate. The liberal intelligentsia appeared to have prevailed and won the support of the regime. This intellectual euphoria was obviously naïve and lacking in nuance, but the Word was undeniably alive and well.

One day I went to the Russian Army House, the pastel blue building on Suvorov Square, to attend the massive posthumous celebration of Pyotr Grigorenko's ninetieth birthday. The Paratroopers' Song and Dance Ensemble performed Russian and Ukrainian folk songs in his honor, and the ceremony was broadcast live on TV. President Yeltsin issued a decree giving him his own museum, a street named after him, and a memorial plaque on his home. Headed by Arseny Roginsky, all the old dissidents sat there in the auditorium and followed along in this rather remarkable event.

A couple of days before I had witnessed an entirely different scene at the Army House: the nationalist poet Sergei Vikulov's seventy-fifth birthday celebration. Sitting in front of me was the notorious "black colonel" Viktor Alksnis. Yury Bondarev, the bilious master of ceremonies, declared that fifth columnists had taken over literature, that there was a Satanic ball going on in Moscow. His elderly colleagues in the audience nodded in approval and applauded. Finally, he began addressing Vikulov as "Pikul," referring to the author of mass-produced patriotic historical novels. The atmosphere felt slightly paranoid, and I couldn't help but think that all these people were simply losers. I was wrong.

At the Russian University of the Humanities I participated in a session with the so-called Mandelstam Society. I was especially pleased to be able to meet the profoundly erudite—and utterly modest—Mikhail Gasparov. When I introduced myself as Nils Åke Nilsson's student, he had a snappy comeback: "So am I!," he quipped.

In Gothenburg I was swamped with work. For a while there were no more trips to Russia. I barely managed to note that Boris Yeltsin at the turn of the millennium had been succeeded by Vladimir Putin.

In 2001 *The Russian Mephisto* came out in Petersburg. Alexander Lavrov had finally reviewed and polished the Russian text. That was the best thing that could have happened. In the spring of 2002 the book was presented at a ceremony in Moscow. The Symbolist scholars Nikolai Kotrelyov and Monika Spivak gave it a very warm reception. Spivak described Medtner as an unbelievably charismatic individual who was everywhere adept at winning over others, both women and men, to his ideas. Paradoxically enough, although he gradually became less and less able to cope with life, he served as a prominent nexus between Russian and German culture and ultimately mirrored an entire epoch.

Aleksei Losev's widow, Professor of Antiquity Aza Takho-Godi, held a presentation at the Glinka Museum and spoke equally generously about my book. I got to know her and her niece Yelena Takho-Godi.

Arseny Roginsky, with Pyotr Grigorenko's portrait, at the Grigorenko celebration in 1997

From then on it became a good tradition of mine to call on them at the Losev House on Old Arbat Street and occasionally participate in their functions. I recalled that once in the 1980s I had attempted to arrange an interview with Losev, but he was very old at the time and had to decline. Yelena and I initiated a friendship that I value highly. A professor of philology, she is also a talented and prize-winning writer of both poetry and prose. We have cooperated to some extent on writing projects connected with Aleksei Losev's early contacts with the Swiss-Russian Erismann family of physicians who also, in fact, had ties to my great-grandfather pathologist Axel Key.

I got to know Yury Davydov through Yakhnina. I had read his articles about the late nineteenth- and early twentieth-century revolutionaries and terrorists in *Ogonyok*. He had just scored a real hit with his 1999 genre-busting documentary novel *Bestseller*, in which the old historian mutates into a postmodernist who allows different temporal planes to meet and overlap. He focuses in particular on the history of duplicity in Russia. He documents Yevno Azef's dual political role, an important background to the fatal interplay of terrorism and tsarism at the heart of *Petersburg*. He interprets Azef's "provocation" as a prelude to Stalin's treachery against everything the nineteenth-century radicals had cherished, discovering the link between these betrayals in the implacable Vladimir Burtsev, who first unmasked Azef and later, in Siberian exile, warned against his fellow prisoner Josef Stalin's brutality and unscrupulousness. Everything was so close to my own interests. In the 1940s, Davydov had served his five years in a camp. Remarkably, however, this experience had not in the least made him cynical or embittered. He confessed to me that he basically trusted every new person he met.

Yakhnina also introduced me to eighty-nine-year-old Alexander Borshchagovsky, a longtime friend of Sweden. I had written about him in *Expressen* in 1964, at which time he was the chairman of the Sweden-Soviet Friendship Association and professed himself an adherent of communism. When we met now, he described Bolshevik ideology as a social cancer. He could look back on the many turns his long life as a Jew had taken. He was born in 1913, at the time of the Beilis trial. In 1921 he witnessed the introduction of a law by the Bolsheviks prohibiting anti-Semitism, but as early as 1936 in his native Ukrainian village he had realized that the pendulum was swinging back. After serving as a reporter on the front in WWII, he returned to a situation in which Judeophobia was again becoming official state policy. Soon came the campaigns, in which he himself was a target. In brief, his life was a mirror of twentieth-century Jewish life in Russia.

Intermarriage is common among Russian intelligentsia families. Borshchagovsky's wife's daughter from a previous marriage, Svetlana Karmalita, wrote the screenplays to several of her husband Aleksei German's films. Aleksei was the son of the writer Yury German, who happened to be Sergei Rittenberg's brother-in-law. Borshchagovsky and I noted that Rittenberg in fact appears briefly in one of the Germans' most acclaimed films, *Khrustalyov, My Car!*, set in Stalin's last years.

In the fall of 2002 I was promoted to full professor of Russian, "with a Concentration in Literature." By that point, after all my training and planning, my research was finally entering a new phase. I launched it at a Russian-Scandinavian symposium in Moscow with a subsequently published paper on the intense lobbying by émigré writers in the struggle for the first Russian Nobel Prize that ended in the election of Ivan Bunin in 1933, and followed up with a number of new articles on Bely, Medtner, Ellis, and Ilyin. At the same time, I began contributing little vignettes on Russian cultural history to *Svenska Dagbladet*.

Retired geologist Abram Blokh soon visited Gothenburg. He was a zealous amateur researcher who had scoured the archives and just published a doorstopper on the theme of Russia and the Nobel Prize that contained a great deal of new material on the Pasternak affair in particular. We went together to call on the legendary, now ninety-eight-year-old poetry expert Erik Mesterton to hear what he had to say about the stubborn rumor in the former Soviet Union that throughout the early 1960s, Akhmatova had been a front-runner in the deliberations of the Nobel committee. Mesterton had met her in Komarovo in the summer of 1962, and he had let slip to friends a comment to the effect that she was a possible candidate, thereby laying the foundation for the speculation. With me acting as his interpreter, Mesterton denied that he had had any sort of mandate from the Swedish Academy at the time. Much later it would transpire that Akhmatova had been of interest in only one year, 1965, and that on that occasion she was passed over for Sholokhov—recommended by the same Mesterton...

In December 2003 I called on Nobel laureate in physics Vitaly Ginzburg at the Grand Hotel in Stockholm and asked him a few questions. The background to my visit was as follows: in the bitterly cold winter of 1942, he and his friend and colleague Yevgeny Feinberg had been evacuated together with their entire institute to Kazan. There, on Feinberg's initiative, they took upon themselves the task of burying Bely's friend Sergei Solovyov, who had just died in a mental hospital and had no near relatives in the city. Actually, the closest was Feinberg himself, who was the brother of Solovyov's son-in-law Ilya, a Pushkin scholar married to Natalya Solovyova. They picked up the body at the morgue, obtained a coffin, hired a reluctant sleigh driver, and with considerable hardship took the deceased to a cemetery outside the city. On the last part of the trip, the driver was going so fast that the young physicists were forced to lie stretched out with their arms wrapped around the coffin to keep it from tumbling off into the snowdrifts. I wondered whether Ginzburg, a confirmed atheist, had been driven by a religious impulse as he lay there holding onto the coffin. He answered firmly in the negative, explaining that there is an ethical impulse within us that is entirely independent of anything having to do with religion. I had probably been hoping that he would in any event remember more, but in fact this memory was lost in a haze, and he could only refer me to his friend Feinberg.

In April 2004 I participated in a second conference about Russian-Scandinavian cultural links in Moscow. I now availed myself of the opportunity to look up Feinberg. He turned out to be a thoroughly likeable ninety-two-year-old who admirably cared for his handicapped daughter, who lived with him. There were portraits of his friends and colleagues on the walls: Lev Landau, Igor Tamm, and Andrei Sakharov. He had lived his entire life wondering how people endured totalitarian society, a topic which he had written on extensively and also discussed with Werner Heisenberg and Sakharov. It turned out that he had a good recollection of Sergei Solovyov's burial. The ground was frozen solid,

Yevgeny Feinberg, with Andrei Sakharov's and Igor Tamm's portraits behind him, in 2004

and it took him and Ginzburg a long time to dig out a grave. Feinberg had also regularly visited Solovyov at the hospital and had calmly endured anti-Semitic diatribes on the part of the sometimes unpredictable Solovyov, who was a Symbolist to the end. Feinberg stood by his atheism as firmly as had Ginzburg, but he admitted that on one occasion he had undergone an inexplicable, purely religious experience: it was at a Bach concert. The impression he gave was one of serenity and wisdom.

The year 2005 witnessed the celebration of the 125th anniversary of Bely's birth in Moscow. At the conference more than fifty invited papers were presented by scholars from twelve different countries. It was an historic moment. Bely, it would seem, had risen to the rank of national classic.

In 2006 my family and I visited the United States. Outside Washington I called on Isaak Babel's ninety-six-year-old widow, Antonina Pirozhkova. She had no trouble going back in time to repeat his sorrowful last words to her as the NKVD took him away: "They didn't let me finish." As for herself, she meant it deeply when she said, "I am fed up with Russia." She would in fact live to be more than one hundred.

Various writers visited us at the Slavic Department. The future Nobel laureate Svetlana Alexievich, an ICORN guest writer in Gothenburg from 2006 to 2008, came and talked about the remarkable method with which she transformed collective interviews into a kind of choral work of art. Lyudmila Petrushevskaya amazed us with her almost frolicsome cheerfulness and verbal play, because her prose is sometimes so gloomy that we expected something quite different. She instructed us in a language she herself had invented and can even use to tell stories, a language with only a slight structural similarity to Russian. It was like a shot in the arm for us.

In the spring of 2009 I published *Twelve Essays on Andrej Bely's "Peterburg,"* a collection of articles written over the years. At the same time, I participated in a Moscow symposium about the Symbolist publishing house Musaget, founded by Emilii Medtner in 1909.

In the fall of 2009 I retired. I was given a farewell party at which I was presented a Festschrift entitled *Symbolism as a World View*. The finest gift I have ever received, it contains contributions from a number of prominent scholars, among them Konstantin Azadovsky, Alexander Lavrov, Nikolai Bogomolov, and Monika Spivak.

In 2010 it was time for a Dostoevsky symposium at the Losev House and a conference at the Bely Museum marking the 130th anniversary of Bely's birth. Bely had grown even bigger. Again there were many papers and a broad international representation. Focusing on Bely's unique breadth, a high-ranking cultural functionary declared that he was something more than just a writer and portrayed him as a prominent Russian philosopher of culture. That sounded good, but it was basically double-edged praise that exploited Symbolism for nationalistic purposes.

In Moscow one day, film producer Yevgeny Gindilis invited me to an elegant lunch. He happened to be closely related to Natalya Venkstern, who I had discovered a few years before was a psychoanalytical patient around the same time as Spielrein. In 1910 she became perhaps the first writer in the world to undergo Freudian therapy. She was directly descended from the son of a Stockholm bookbinder who had been captured at the Battle of Lesnaya in 1708 and later entered the Russian military. And that was not all. She moved in Symbolist circles and was a childhood friend of Sergei Solovyov (who also underwent analysis at an

Konstantin Azadovsky, myself, and Alexander Lavrov, in 2009

early stage). Eventually, she became rather well known as a writer of books for young people. Her healing process appears to be described in a case study presented in the deep-psychology journal *Psikhoterapiya* in 1914. Over lunch, Gindilis lamented the fact that I had never had an opportunity to meet his prematurely deceased father, who first worked as a psychiatrist in Moscow and then emigrated to the United States via Israel. After I had thought about it for a while it struck me that I had in fact met the man that evening in the spring of 1983 at Vyacheslav Ivanov's. It was with him that I had discussed Spielrein and coercive psychiatry in the Soviet Union. The world of the Russian intelligentsia is indeed small. Ivanov was and is married to Lev Kopelev's stepdaughter. Kopelev himself was a very close friend of Yevgeny Gindilis's father, Viktor.

After returning home from Moscow, I wrote an article in *Expressen* attacking the hardened anti-Semitic and nationalist writer Israel Shamir, who together with his son, whose mother is Swedish, was supporting Julian Assange, the suddenly world-famous founder of Wikileaks. In a series of contributions, I gradually raised doubts about Assange himself, who had close ties to the Russian Judeophobe and had ultimately fallen prey to his conspiracy theories. My introductory article attracted international attention.

In 2012 I published in Swedish a collection of popular studies connected by way of Bely's novel that recapitulated many of the themes of my research. Translated into English as *Poetry and Psychiatry: Essays on Early Twentieth-Century Russian Symbolist Culture*, it came out in the United States in 2014. I also felt that the time was ripe for a more ambitious summary, and so Hans Åkerström and I brought out a bibliography of works in various formats dealing with *Petersburg*. Our list of studies and extensive annotations to the novel currently runs to more than eight hundred items. When I began, I could almost count them on the fingers of one hand.

Petersburg is a rebus that I have attempted to solve from different angles. At the same time, alongside Grossman's *Life and Fate*, my greatest reading experience has been a novel whose narrative form is far from Bely's own, namely Solzhenitsyn's *Cancer Ward*, which teems with life in the very waiting room of death.

In the spring and fall of 2013 I participated in two major conferences on the history of psychoanalysis in Russia and on the musical Medtner family in Petersburg and Moscow, respectively. I was greeted by a Russia under Vladimir Putin that was already gorging itself on nationalism. It felt ominous.

The conference on Freud and Russia was arranged from Izhevsk, the capital of the Udmurt Republic. Intense research there on the subject has resulted in documentation and published translations of old forgotten original works. Freud in Izhevsk—the Russian idealism one senses here is almost touching.

In connection with the Medtner conference—which was divided between the Glinka Museum and the Bely Museum, since it dealt equally with the composer Nikolai and his brother Emilii—I became acquainted with Vitaly Shentalinsky, who happens to be married to a relative of the Medtners. But he is also responsible for three huge volumes documenting the suffering writers endured under Stalin and describes abuses whose full extent was previously unknown. In Shentalinsky I met a living Russian intellectual who in my opinion has accomplished a scholarly exploit.

In the summer of 2014 I attended a Bely conference organized by the Anthroposophists in Dornach. It was the first time (after preparatory work by Thomas Beyer) that they opened the door to their archive collections, which contain in particular unknown letters.

A time is approaching for Russia that is in fact more like a previous age. Everything we believed in is being forfeited. *Day of the Oprichnik*, Vladimir Sorokin's satirical future vision from 2006, seems to be on the way to becoming reality. A senseless war in Ukraine has succeeded the illegal annexation of Crimea.

Today the old grandiose neurotic Ivan Ilyin has become a political guru. This is very sinister. I remember how I sat there alone in a Moscow archive and celebrated the hundredth anniversary of his birth in 1983. I never could have dreamed that this unfortunate patient of Freud's living in the diaspora would one day regain a place in the Kremlin (where he had in fact grown up, the grandson of the commandant). For a time in German exile in the 1930s, he made common cause with Joseph Goebbels. Little and large merge in almost Gogolian fashion, as a political fool is transformed into a national lodestar, something I have written about in *Dagens Nyheter*.

In the fall of 2015 I attended the Stanford conference marking the 125th anniversary of Boris Pasternak's birth organized by the dynamic Lazar Fleishman, with whom I had done some exciting research on the prelude to Pasternak's Nobel Prize. Bely's 135th birthday was celebrated later that same year in Moscow.

In the middle of the Bely event, we made a little outing to Kuchino, where Bely lived for several important years in the Soviet period, to witness the unveiling of a statue of the hero of the occasion. We refrained the whole time from talking about politics, but finally one of the Russian delegates could not hold back any longer. He stressed how close Symbolism was to Europe and took the liberty of criticizing the Kremlin's attempts to isolate Russia and demarcate some sort of "Eurasian" national identity. He was greeted with applause and considerable assent.

Through the years I have gladly returned to the theme of Sweden and Russia. Because Russia has evidently become a part of me, I am drawn to the historical points of contact between the two countries.

Just now, things seem gloomier than they have for a long time. Experience has taught me, however, that we must never give up—there is always another Russia that offers resistance.

Index

A

Admoni, Vladimir 72
Aitmatov, Chingiz 52
  Day Lasts More Than a Hundred Years, The 52
Aivazovsky, Ivan 57
Akhmatova, Anna 4, 12, 18, 21–22, 29, 39, 58, 72, 85–86
Aksyonov, Vasily 4
  Ticket to the Stars 4
Alexievich, Svetlana 88
Alfredson, Hans 11
Alksnis, Viktor 82
Andropov, Yury 50, 52
Anichkov, Igor 26
Apetyan, Zarui 66
Arnér, Sivar 23–24
Assange, Julian 90
Astakhova, Polina 5
Averintsev, Sergei 57
Azadovsky, Konstantin 15, 50, 88–89
Azef, Yevno 84

B

Babadzhan, Venyamin 30
Babel, Isaak 87
Babi Yar 1
Bach, Johann Sebastian 87
Bakhmin, Vyacheslav 73
Balmont, Konstantin 48
Beatles 2
Beilis, Menahem Mendel 44, 84
Bekhterev, Vladimir 49, 68, 74, 76
Bekhtereva, Natalya 74–75
Bellman, Carl Michael 28–29

Bely, Andrei 6–8, 12, 17–29, 31, 36–37, 50, 52, 54, 57, 65, 67, 71–72, 81, 85–91
  Petersburg 6, 8, 12, 19, 36–37, 41, 49, 72, 84, 90
Berberova, Nina 12, 41, 65–66, 71
Bergman, Ingmar 45
  Silence, The 45
Beriya, Lavrenty 72
Bernadsky, Sergei 16
Bertolucci, Bernardo 73
Bettelheim, Bruno 56
Beyer, Thomas 91
Binswanger, Ludwig 44
Björkegren, Hans 73
Block, Bertil 2
Blok, Alexander 2, 39, 41, 52, 57, 71
Blokh, Abram 85
Blomqvist, Lars Erik 12–14, 16, 18, 20, 24, 26, 69, 73
  Soviet Union Looks Back, The 16
Bloodless Murder, The
Bobrov, Sergei 21
Bogoraz, Larisa 32, 36, 61, 73
Boguslavskaya, Zoya 20
Boky, Gleb 77
Böll, Heinrich 21, 31
Bondarev, Yury 82
Bonner, Yelena 42, 50, 59, 69, 79
  Mothers and Daughters 79–80
Borshchagovskaya, Valentina 85
Borshchagovsky, Alexander 84–85
Brel, Jacques 8
Brezhnev, Leonid 13, 27, 29, 33, 41, 43–44, 46
Brik, Lili 19–20

Brodsky, Iosif 7, 15, 22
Bryusov, Valery 49
Bukovsky, Vladimir 7, 13, 26, 31–32, 34–36, 42
　Report from the Red House 26
Bulgakov, Mikhail 19, 24, 30
　Master and Margarita, The 19, 24, 69
Bunin, Ivan 7, 85
Burtsev, Vladimir 84
Butyrka Prison 79
Bykov, Dmitry 8, 10

C
Carl XVI Gustaf 50
Ceaușescu, Nicolae 31
Chekhov, Anton 25
　Cherry Orchard, The 25
Chernenko, Konstantin 66
Chertkov, Leonid 49
Chistopol 22
Chronicle of Current Events 15, 43, 59, 65
Chukovskaya, Lydia 20, 22, 32, 66
　Deserted House, The 22
Chukovsky, Kornei 22
Corvalán, Luis 36

D
Dagens Nyheter 3, 35, 72, 79, 91
Daniel, Alexander 59–60
Daniel, Yuly 7–8, 10, 13, 23–24, 48, 59, 61
Davydov, Yury 83
　Bestseller 83
Denikin, Anton 4
Dobin, Yefim 29, 31
Dobychin, Leonid 29
Dolgopolov, Leonid 37, 67, 72
Dolmatovsky, Yevgeny 4, 7, 12
　"A Nightmare" 5
Donne, John 15
Dornach 7, 12, 17, 72, 91
Dostoevsky, Aleksei 38
Dostoevsky, Dmitry 38
Dostoevsky, Fyodor 4, 12, 38, 68, 88
　Idiot, The 12
　Brothers Karamazov, The 19
Dugin, Alexander 80
Dylan, Bob 2

E
Eckermann, Johann Peter 21–22
　Conversations with Goethe 21
Ehrenburg, Ilya 5, 12
Eichenwald, Yury 59–60
　Don Quixote on Russian Soil 60
Eisenstein, Sergei 19
Ekholm, Jan 63
Ellis 72, 85
Encyclopedia of Philosophy 57
Enquist, Per Olov 24
Erdman, Nikolai 69
Erismanns 84
Expressen 2–4, 6, 8, 10, 12, 23–24, 26, 35–36, 41–42, 46, 48, 56, 67, 69, 84, 90

F
Falk, Arvid 23–25
Feinberg, Yevgeny 86–87
Feniks 7
Fioletov, Anatoly 30
Fleishman, Lazar 91
France, Anatole 26
Freud, Anna 52
Freud, Sigmund 44–45, 48–49, 52–53, 64–66, 69, 81, 88, 90–91
Frumkina, Natalya 63
Fyodorova, Alexandra 38–39

G
Gagen-Torn, Nina 18, 27–28
Galich, Alexander 36
Gasparov, Mikhail 82
Gedin, Per 8, 11
Gellerstein, Solomon 56
German, Aleksei 85
　Khrustalyov, My Car! 85
German, Yury 85
Gindilis, Viktor 53, 89
Gindilis, Yevgeny 88–89
Ginzburg, Vitaly 86–87
Gippius, Zinaida 44, 66
Goebbels, Joseph 91
Goethe, Johann Wolfgang 21
　Faust 35
Gogol, Nikolai 20, 91
Goldman, Emma 78

Goncharova, Natalya   19
Gorbachev, Mikhail   54, 61, 67, 69, 73, 75
Gorbacheva, Raisa   73
Gorbatov, Alexander   6
   Years off My Life   6
Gorky, Maksim   31, 52, 60, 81
   Song of the Stormy Petrel, The   60
Göteborgs-Posten   26
Graan, Jonny   9
Granin, Daniil   26
Grechishkin, Sergei   29, 37
Grigorenko, Pyotr   27, 33–35, 69, 81, 83
Grigorenko, Zinaida   69
Grossman, Vasily   49–50, 90
   Life and fate   49, 90
Guberman, Igor   48–49
Gumilyov, Nikolai   39
Gustafsson, Bo   35
Gustafsson, Lars   25

H

Hammer, Armand   64
Heisenberg, Werner   86
Heller, Frank   76
Herbstman, Alexander   49
   Reflections of Lightning   49
Hitler, Adolf   50, 55, 71

I

Ilyin, Ivan   44, 51–52, 85, 91
Ingdahl, Kazimiera   34, 47, 62, 64, 66
Ionesco, Eugène   61
   Rhinosceros   61
Ivanov, Vyacheslav Ivanovich   17–18, 39
Ivanov, Vyacheslav Vsevolodovich   52–53, 89
Ivnev, Ryurik   21

J

Jung, Carl Gustav   37, 44, 51, 53, 57, 64, 80–81
Jung, Franz   80

K

Kafka, Franz   15
Kaledin, Sergei   73
Kamenev, Lev   25

Karmalita, Svetlana   85
Kasaravetsky, Vladimir   18
Kashpirovsky, Anatoly   75
Kataev, Valentin   66–67
Katanyan, Vasily   20
Kauchcisvili, Nina   67
Kedrina, Zoya   48
Kennedy, John F.   2
Key, Axel   84
KGB   15–16, 18, 20, 27, 35, 41, 60, 64, 69, 75
Khardzhiev, Nikolai   18, 57–58
Kharms, Daniil   12, 58
Khlebnikov, Velimir   58, 68
Khmelnitskaya, Tamara   17–18, 27, 64
Khodasevich, Vladislav   65–66
Khrushchev, Nikita   2, 4, 6, 56
Kierkegaard, Soren   49
Kiselyov, Yury   59–60
Kobylinsky, Lev see Ellis
Kollontai, Alexandra   30, 48
Kolyma   27, 50
Komech, Aleksei   51
Kontinent   27
Kopelev, Lev   20–21, 31–32, 35, 89
Kornilov, Lavr   59
Kotrelyov, Nikolai   82
Kropotkin, Pyotr   78
Kudasheva-Cuvillier, Maya   48
Kudrova, Irma   72
Kunyaev, Stanislav   11
Kushner, Alexander   64
Kuzmin, Mikhail   25
Kvant   59

L

Landau, Lev   86
Latynina, Larisa   5
Lavrin, Janko   68–70
Lavrov, Alexander   29, 37, 39, 67, 82, 88–89
Lenin, Vladimir   8, 43–44, 71
Lermontov, Mikhail   39
Levinton, Georgy   64
Ligachev, Yegor   73
Literaturnaya gazeta   4, 26, 48
Literaturnoe nasledstvo   57
Litvinov, Maxim   32

Litvinova, Tatyana   32
Lorentzon, Emi   48
Losev, Aleksei   82, 84
Lövgren, Jan   4
Lubyanka Prison   6, 50, 79
Lunacharsky, Anatoly   25
Luria, Alexander   53
Luria, Yelena   53
Lyubimov, Yury   69

M

Maksimov, Dmitry   12, 25–26, 36, 64
Malevich, Kazimir   19, 58
Malmgren, Finn   30
Mandelstam, Osip   2, 5, 21, 30, 58
Manuilov, Viktor   39
Mao Zedong   12
Marchenko, Anatoly   61
Marshak, Samuil   3
Márton, Elisabeth   81
Martov, Yuly   71
Marxistiskt Forum   35
Masaryk, Tomáš   68
Mayakovsky, Vladimir   18–20, 39, 58, 79
Medtner, Emilii   37, 43–45, 50, 52, 60, 69, 72–73, 79–82, 85, 88, 90
Medtner, Nikolai   90
Medvedev, Roy   31
Mehr, Hjalmar   5
Mehr, Liselotte   5
Meilakh, Mikhail   64–65
Mekler, Yury   16, 18
Melior, Yekaterina   17, 39
Mesterton, Erik   85–86
Meyerhold, Vsevolod   19–20
Michnik, Adam   73
Milgrom, Ida   43
Miller, Arthur   73
Mindlin, Emil   29–30
   Unusual Interlocutors   30
Modigliani, Amedeo   18
Montreux   12
Muratova, Kseniya   37

N

Nabokov, Vladimir   12, 16
Nadezhdina, Nadezhda   3
Napoleon   46
Nappelbaum, Ida   39–40, 65, 71

Narbut, Vladimir   47
Naritsa, Mikhail   2
Nashe obshchee delo   3–4
Nechkina, Militsa   54
Neizvestny, Ernst   41
Nekrasov, Viktor   36
New Age, The   68
New York Review of Books   56
Nikolskaya, Tatyana   39
Nilsson, Nils Åke   1–2, 4–6, 73, 82
   Soviet Russian Literature   1
Nixon, Richard   33
NKVD   17, 27, 48, 69, 87
Nobile, Umberto   30
Novoe vremya   68

O

OBERIU   64
Obleukhov, Dmitry   49
Odoevtseva, Irina   25, 39
   On the Banks of the Neva   25
Ogonyok   84
Oksman, Yulian   3–5
Okudzhava, Bulat   8–12, 45–46, 62
   Extraordinary Adventures of Secret Agent Shipov, The   46
   Good Luck, Schoolboy!   9
   Meeting with Bonaparte, The   46
   Merry Drummer, The   10–11
Okudzhava, Olga   10
Olesha, Olga   38
Olesha, Yury   38, 66
   Envy   66
Orage, Alfred Richard   68
Ord & Bild   1
Origo   2, 4
Orlova, Raisa   21
Orlovsky, Ernst   75
Österåker Prison   73

P

Palach, Jan   25
Pankeev, Konstantin   48, 52
Pankeev, Sergei (Wolfman)   48
Panteleev, Leonid   29
Parnis, Alexander   48, 68
Pasternak, Boris   7, 18, 21, 32, 73–74, 85, 91
   Doctor Zhivago   18

Peredelkino   19–20, 22, 32, 37, 66–67, 74, 76, 78
Perestroika   69
Perris, Carlo   26
Pervomaisky, Leonid   5
Petrov, Sergei   27–28
Petrushevskaya, Lyudmila   88
Pirozhkova, Antonina   87
Piskunov, Vladimir   31
Platonov, Andrei   30
Plisetskaya, Maya   20
Pluchek, Valentin   20
Plyushch, Leonid   35
Popov, Gavriil   66
Posev   7
Prokhanov, Alexander   80
Psikhoterapiya   89
Pushkin, Alexander   8, 54, 69, 79, 86
   Eugene Onegin   19
Putin, Vladimir   82, 90

R
Rapoport, Yakov   76–77
Ratushinskaya, Irina   67
Razgon, Lev   77–78
Rittenberg, Sergei   4, 41, 85
Rode, Gunars   42, 67
Rode, Ieva   42
Roginsky, Arseny   36, 50, 63, 82–83
Roginsky, Boris   63
Rolland, Romain   48
Roosevelt, Eleanor   59
Rozhdestvensky, Robert   11
Russkaya Mysl   25, 41
Ryabushinsky, Stepan   81
Rybakov, Anatoly   42, 67
   Children of the Arbat, The   67
   Heavy Sand   42
Rysk bokrevy (Russian Book Review)   12–13, 19
Rysk kulturrevy (Russian Cultural Review)   13, 24, 30

S
Sakharov, Andrei   31–32, 34, 42, 50, 52, 59, 69, 80, 86–87
Samizdat   5, 7, 13, 15, 26–27, 59, 61, 67
Saraskina, Lyudmila   79
Sarmakesheva, Natalya   61–63, 66

Sarnov, Benedikt   22
Sartre Jean-Paul   41
Scando-Slavica   27
Schmidt, Otto   81
Schmidt, Vera   81
Schmidt, Vladimir   81
Seraphim (Sarovsky), St.   26
Sfinksy   7
Shaginyan, Marietta   37, 43–45, 48, 71
   Hydrocentral   44
   The Ulyanov Family   44
Shalamov, Varlam   27
Shamir, Israel   89
Shcharansky, Anatoly   43
Shchedrin, Rodion   20
Shentalinsky, Vitaly   91
Shervinsky, Sergei   48
Shestov, Lev   15
Shikhanovich, Yuri   59–60, 65
Shklovsky, Viktor   18–19, 45–47
   Energy of Delusion: A Book on Plot   47
   Zoo   46
Sholokhov, Mikhail   4, 7, 10, 22, 86
Silberstein, Ilya   57
Silman, Tamara   72
Simonov, Konstantin   37
Sinyavsky, Andrei   7–8, 10, 13, 23–24, 36, 48
Slavinsky, Yefim   15
Slonim, Ilya   32
Slutsky, Boris   21
Smirnova, Engelina   65
Sofronov, Anatoly   2
Solidarity   43, 56, 61
Solovyov, Sergei   22–23, 39, 72, 86–88
Solovyova, Natalya   86
Solovyova, Olga   22–23, 39
Solzhenitsyn, Alexander   1, 3, 20–27, 29, 31–35, 44, 63, 73, 90
   Cancer Ward   90
   First Circle, The   21
   Gulag Archipelago, The   23, 27, 32
   "Live not by Lies"   27, 64
   One Day in the Life of Ivan Denisovich   1
Sorokin, Vladimir   91
   Day of the Oprichnik   91

Soviet Protest: The New Russian Opposition in Documents 13
Spielrein, Isaak 53, 56
Spielrein, Menikha 53–56, 81
Spielrein, Rakhil 56
Spielrein, Sabina 53, 81, 88–89
Spielrein, Jan 56
Spivak, Monika 82, 88
Starchik, Pyotr 59
Steiner, Rudolf 38
Sternberg, Lev 28
Stockholms-Tidningen 3
Strindberg, August 17, 23
   Occult Diary, The 17
   Red Room, The 23
Strömstedt, Bo 2, 24
Struve, Gleb 5, 37, 41
Struve, Pyotr 41
Stalin, Iosif 1–3, 32–33, 38, 43–44, 48–49, 54–56, 59, 71, 74, 76, 78, 84–85, 91
Summer Lightning 48
Superfin, Gabriel 48
Suslov, Mikhail 44
Svenska Dagbladet 73, 85
Symbolism as a World View 88
Syrokomsky, Vitaly 26

T
Takho-Godi, Aza 82
Takho-Godi, Yelena 82
Tamm, Igor 56, 86–87
Tarasova, Vera 45, 51
Taratuta, Yevgeniya 78–79
Tarkovsky, Arseny 12
Tarsis, Valery 2, 6
Terapiano, Yury 25
Thaw 2, 4, 6, 69
Tolstoy, Lev 42, 46, 59, 68
   War and Peace 19
Tolstoy, Lev Jr. 21, 42
Toporov, Vladimir 52, 54
Treblinka 50
Trifonov, Yury 42–43
   Another Life 43
Tsvetaeva, Anastasia 58
Tsvetaeva, Marina 21–22, 30, 58, 72
   Youth, The 30

Turgeneva, Asya 7, 12
Tynyanov, Yury 17

V
Vaginov, Konstantin 38
Venkstern, Natalya 88
Vigdorova, Frida 22
Vikulov, Sergei 82
Voloshin, Maksimilian 29, 37, 48
Voznesensky, Andrei 20, 73
Vul, Leonid Davidovich 59
Vul, Leonid Davydovich 59
Vysotsky, Vladimir 50–51, 57, 69
Vzdornov, Gerold 65

W
Wallenberg, Raoul 60
Wästberg, Per 24
Weil, Boris 42, 50
Weil, Lyudmila 50
Weininger, Otto 66
Wenckstern, Jacob (Venkstern, Yakov) 88
Westerlund, Ernst 42
Westerlund, Dora 42

Y
Yakhnina, Yuliana 71, 73, 76–78, 84
Yankov, Ilya 63
Yankov, Vadim 61–62, 66
Yankova, Anastasia 62–63
Yasnaya Polyana 42
Yeltsin, Boris 51, 79, 81–82
Yesenin, Sergei 34
Yesenin-Volpin, Alexander 2, 7
Yevtushenko, Yevgeny 1–3, 7–9, 11–12, 67, 73–75
Yudaism without Embellishment 5

Z
Zaitsev, Boris 25
Zamyatin, Yevgeny 39
Zdanevich, Ilya 68
Zederbaums 72
Zinoviev, Alexander 43
   Yawning Heights 43
Zoshchenko, Mikhail 38
Zoshchenko, Vera 38
Zvezda 29

www.ingramcontent.com/pod-product-compliance
Lightning Source LLC
Chambersburg PA
CBHW050033090426
42735CB00022B/3472